Brotherly Community

The Highest Command of Love

Brotherly Community

The Highest Command of Love

Andreas Ehrenpreis

Claus Felbinger

Introduction by Robert Friedmann

PLOUGH PUBLISHING HOUSE

Published by Plough Publishing House
Walden, New York
Robertsbridge, England
Elsmore, Australia
www.plough.com

10-digit ISBN: 0-87486-190-x
13-digit ISBN: 978-087486-190-7

A catalog record for this book is available from the British Library.
Library of Congress Cataloging-in-Publication Data

Ehrenpreis, Andreas, 1589–1662.
  Brotherly community—the highest command of love.
  PARTIAL CONTENTS: Ehrenpreis, A. An epistle on brotherly
community as the highest command of love.
—Felbinger. C. Confession of faith addressed to the Council of
Landshut, 1560.
  1. Hutterite Brethren—Doctrinal and controversial works.
I. Felbinger, Klaus, d. 1560, joint author. II. Ehrenpreis, Andreas,
1589–1662. An epistle on brotherly community as the highest
command of love. 1978. III. Felbinger, Klaus, d. 1560. Confession
of faith addressed to the Council of Landshut, 1560. 1978. IV. Title.
BX8129.H8E38   230'.9'73   78-21065
ISBN 0-87486-190-x

CONTENTS

PREFACE

"How can the old structures of injustice be transformed? By spreading the new structures. Jesus announces a new social order.... You can change structures by *being* the messianic community, by *being* the new, just structure."[1] These words were spoken in 1977; but the same question was asked in Jesus' time and in movements of the Spirit throughout the centuries: "Men and brothers, what shall we do?"

Our interest in publishing two Anabaptist documents in one book is not primarily a scholarly one. Rather our hope is to offer a clear answer for those who ask that vital question today.

Andreas Ehrenpreis and Claus Felbinger, writing in 1650 and 1560, were both "touched by the Spirit," to use Robert Friedmann's words. They were both members of the Anabaptist Christian communities called Hutterian, the former an Elder, the latter a Servant of the Word who suffered martyrdom. Together they give an

[1] Larry Miller, "What Does 'Peace Church' Mean?" From Church and Peace Steering Committee Meeting, Versailles, October 1977.

vii

impassioned witness to a life of discipleship of Jesus and brotherly love in community, led by the Spirit.

This witness was read with enthusiasm in the twentieth century by another man moved by the same Spirit, Eberhard Arnold.[1] Here were expressed centuries ago the very ideas—revolutionary ideas—that he was putting into practice in the present.

Eberhard Arnold's decision in 1907 to follow Jesus regardless of the consequences had already led him to gather together, in Germany in 1920, a small group of brothers and sisters who were committed to a life of full surrender to God's will. This community was based on the Sermon on the Mount and the account in Acts 2 and 4. They lived in total sharing, full community of goods—the direct outcome of love. "Community filled with Jesus Christ is automatically pushed to share everything."[2] And Andreas Ehrenpreis, a brother in the Spirit, spoke the same truth across the centuries. What an encouragement for today too, a pattern for the new social order, the new, just structure!

Eberhard Arnold had never wanted an isolated

[1] Eberhard Arnold, 1883–1935. See *The Mennonite Encyclopedia*, vol. I, pp. 162–164. For more about Eberhard Arnold and the *Bruderhof*, see list of publications by the Plough Publishing House.
[2] Jacques Langhart, "What Does 'Community' Mean?" From Church and Peace Steering Committee Meeting, Versailles, October 1977.

movement. His early studies had acquainted him with the Baptizers' movement of the sixteenth and seventeenth centuries and the Hutterian *Bruderhofs* in Moravia. It cannot have been anything but a leading of the Spirit that brought him face to face with the realization in 1921 that the Hutterian communities or *Bruderhofs* (to which Andreas Ehrenpreis and Claus Felbinger had belonged) still existed in the twentieth century in Canada and the United States. Several brothers had even suffered as martyrs in World War I. He felt the added authority these Anabaptist documents acquire when placed in the context of four hundred years of Hutterian community life, beginning in 1528 and continuing almost uninterruptedly up to the present day, though at times severely persecuted.

It was through a letter from Robert Friedmann in Vienna, in 1926, that Eberhard Arnold obtained the address of an Elder of the Hutterian Church in Canada, the late Elias Walter. From him Eberhard Arnold received in 1927 a copy of Andreas Ehrenpreis's epistle and printed it in 1928 in a powerful condensed version. In 1930 Eberhard Arnold visited the *Bruderhofs* in North America. The little German *Bruderhof* was fully incorporated into the Hutterian Church during that visit, and he himself was ordained as its Servant of the Word.

He returned to Germany, on fire to print more Anabaptist writings, many of which had been given to him by the American brothers. Claus Felbinger's Confession was copied by Eberhard Arnold's daughter-in-law Edith from a sixteenth-century handwritten codex in the Central Library of Zurich and prepared for print. But with the rise of Nazism it was never printed in Germany. The reason is made strikingly clear by Claus Felbinger himself: the States of this world and the Churches of this world are incompatible with the new social order of the Kingdom of God and the Church of the Body of Christ.

We are glad to offer both these documents here (in reverse chronological order) after reworking the old translations in an attempt to bring the language closer to modern English. The earlier translations had been made around 1940 by the Hutterian Society of Brothers and published by *The Mennonite Quarterly Review* in October 1960 and April 1955 respectively. Robert Friedmann's introductions have been gratefully included, with a few omissions and slight alterations. In Robert Friedmann the Anabaptist cause found not only a thorough scholar, but also a warm and discerning friend.[1]

We hope that the same Spirit who inspired these documents in 1650 and 1560 will speak again through them today to those who are willing to give everything for a new, just structure. The lives of these three men, Andreas Ehrenpreis, Claus Felbinger, and Eberhard Arnold, among many others, can truly be said to have borne fruits of the

[1] Robert Friedmann, 1891–1970. See also *The Mennonite Quarterly Review,* April 1974.

Spirit that are still alive and flourishing today. May the Spirit continue to spread this message and multiply its fruits!

October 1978   *The Editors*

ANDREAS EHRENPREIS

An Epistle on
Brotherly Community
as the
Highest Command
of Love

1650

INTRODUCTION[1]

The teachings and other writings of the Hutterian Brothers have always stressed community of goods as the outcome of love in action. The way of total surrender of property and sharing of all goods still is considered the highest command for anyone who wants to follow Christ and be His disciple.

When in 1545 the Gabrielite Brothers decided to join the Hutterites in Moravia, conversations were held to formulate the basic principles upon which such a fusion would be achieved. The result was a document called *Die fünf Artikel des größten Streites zwischen uns und der Welt.*[2]

[1] This introduction is abridged and slightly adapted from the article by Robert Friedmann, "An Epistle Concerning Communal Life. A Hutterite Manifesto of 1650 and Its Modern Paraphrase," *The Mennonite Quarterly Review,* October 1960, pp. 249–254.

[2] A.J.F.Zieglschmid, *Die älteste Chronik der Hutterischen Brüder* (Philadelphia, 1943), pp. 269–316.

Later, about 1577, it was reworked by Peter Walpot (who at that time was the Elder of the Hutterian Bruderhofs in Moravia) and shaped into the document known as "The Great Article Book," whose third Article deals at great length with the principle of community of goods.[1]

After their expulsion from Moravia in 1622, the Hutterian Brotherhood experienced a sharp decline. The old missionary spirit waned, and life in Slovakia during the Thirty Years' War and the Turkish attacks was so hard that the old discipline began to slacken. At this critical moment there arose in their midst a leader of truly great stature—Andreas Ehrenpreis (1589–1662). Elected in 1621 as Servant of the Word, actual leader of the Church from 1630, and its Elder from 1639, this unusual man achieved almost as much as Jakob Hutter or Peter Rideman one hundred years earlier.

Ehrenpreis, born of Württemberg stock

[1] Peter Walpot, 1519–1578. *Das Große Artikelbuch* (1577), pp. 59–317, *Quellen zur Geschichte der Täufer,* XII; *Glaubenszeugniße oberdeutscher Taufgesinnter,* II, ed. Robert Friedmann (Heidelberg: Gütersloher Verlagshaus Gerd Mohn, 1967).

on a Hutterian Bruderhof in Moravia, by profession a miller, set himself to the almost impossible task of redressing the decline and reviving the old Brotherhood along its time-honored lines of strict community of goods, discipline, nonresistance, and the spirit of brotherly love and discipleship.

Among his many writings still extant (both in European libraries and among the Hutterian Brothers and the Hutterian Society of Brothers in Canada and the US) one document stands out in particular: his *Sendbrief an alle diejenigen, so sich rühmen und bedünken lassen, daß sie ein abgesondertes Volk von der Welt sein wollen... brüderliche Gemeinschaft, das höchste Gebot der Liebe, betreffend.* We may assume that it was written some time before 1650, when missioners were sent from Slovakia to visit Switzerland and possibly also parts of Western Germany to spread the message of the brotherly life. That the letter was primarily drawn up with missionary intentions can be seen in part from its contents (for instance, the Swiss are mentioned and Menno Simons's widely read *Fundament-Buch* is quoted). In 1652 Ehrenpreis had his *Sendbrief* printed as a booklet, and we must assume that he intended it both for home use and for promotional purposes.

Copies of the *Sendbrief* must have been in existence throughout the following centuries. In 1920 Elias Walter, an outstanding Elder of the Hutterian Brothers in Canada, decided that it would serve the Brotherhood well to have this *Sendbrief* printed again. Thus a book of 189 pages was produced, with the notice *"aufs Neue herausgegeben von den Hutterischen Brüdern in Amerika, 1920. Scottdale, Pa.,"* which found a fairly wide distribution. In 1955 it was reprinted again in Canada.

In the Germany of post World War I the soil seemed to have been ready for a beginning similar to that in Moravia around 1530. Eberhard Arnold (1883–1935), who felt the urgent need of a community settlement built on radical Christian foundations, gathered around him in 1920 a small circle of people who were ready to return to the ways of the early Church. Out of this small beginning grew the Rhön Bruderhof near Fulda in central Germany, which was set up very similarly to a Hutterian Bruderhof in Moravia four centuries ago. But it was only afterwards that Eberhard Arnold heard of the Hutterian Brothers in America and of their Elder Elias Walter, and that he discovered he was standing unwittingly in a great historic tradition. He was eager to build the Rhön Bruderhof on ever deeper foundations, and it was not his intention to establish a separate organization or create a group of followers for himself. He was therefore strongly moved to seek contact with the Hutterian Brothers in North America through their Elder Elias Walter, who sent him the Ehrenpreis *Sendbrief* in its 1920 edition.

Understandably, Eberhard Arnold was captivated by this fine document. But for readers in modern Germany it was somewhat too long and betrayed its seventeenth-century style. So he undertook the task of rewriting the book and adapting it to the needs of the time, though retaining the flavor of the original. He condensed it drastically, using only pages 1–133 and omitting the last section of the *Sendbrief* (1920 edition, pp. 133–154). He also left out the appendix, which treats the plan of union between the Hutterites and Swiss Brethren in 1557. The new version thus represents roughly half of the original *Sendbrief*. In this fashion an almost contemporary work grew out of this old Hutterian document, summing up in briefest form the motives and arguments for this radical form of Christian living. In 1928, this new version was published by Eberhard Arnold in his magazine *Die Wegwarte* under the title, *Andreas Ehrenpreis, Ein Sendbrief über brüderliche Gemeinschaft, das Höchste Gebot der Liebe betreffend. Neu ins heutige Deutsch in Kürzung übertragen.*[1]

Andreas Ehrenpreis recognized *love* as the very core of the idea of communal

[1] Translators' Note: Our present translation is a reworking of an English version produced several years ago by the Hutterian Society of Brothers and published by Robert Friedmann. See footnote 1, page 1.

living. "Where there is no community there is no true love." Love requires sharing: life in community is the fulfillment of love. The opposite of love and sharing is greed (*Geiz*). All who live in community do this for love alone. Into this framework of loving, brotherly sharing, Ehrenpreis places the ancient and beautiful symbolism of the bread and wine on the Lord's Table. This allegory appeared for the first time in the *Didache* (the "Teaching of the Twelve Apostles") in the second century.[1] As each grain of wheat has to give up its individuality in order to become bread, and as each single grape has to yield its juice to the whole to become wine (and any grain or grape that resists will be discarded), in just the same way each member of the fellowship of the Lord's Table has to yield his self-will in order to become a real part of the entire Church. Ehrenpreis also refers to the Pauline teaching that the natural man in us has to die so that we may find new birth with Christ.

[1] Eberhard Arnold, *The Early Christians after the Death of the Apostles,* selected and edited from all the sources of the first centuries, 2nd ed. (Rifton, NY: Plough Publishing House, 1972), pp. 181–189.

Ehrenpreis was untiring in seeking to convince the Brotherhood of the inescapable need for full community of goods if the Church was to fulfill its purpose, namely that of following Christ's command and being a Church of disciples.

October 1960   *Robert Friedmann*

EPISTLE

A great deal of writing and reporting has been done about community of goods, but so far it has not produced many visible results. Two reasons account for this: the one has to do with community life being based on leaving behind all worldly possessions; the other has to do with obedience, which consists in the surrender of our free will or self-will.[1] Without these steps, perfection cannot be reached. Jesus showed the rich young man this way as the highest demand of love, as the door through which it is hard to go. And yet this is how it must be. It cannot be otherwise. Whoever wants the most precious jewel, the hidden treasure, must sell all that he has—everything—and give it up.

Matt. 13:44

A powerful and undeniable example of this work of the Holy Spirit was the first

---

[1] It cannot be emphasized enough that this surrender is to Jesus only, and not to any man.

Church at Jerusalem. These first Christians had community by selling their houses, lands, and goods and laying the proceeds before the apostles. So no one could say of his goods that they belonged to him. No, they held everything in common. That is an undeniable fact. That is the light that penetrates through the world. That is the invincible City on the Hill; it cannot be hidden.

Matt.
5:14

Now let us think of Jesus in His poverty and remember that the disciple should not be different from his master. Or let us think of sailors who run into danger with an overladen ship; they must lighten the ship and throw their merchandise overboard. How much more must we unburden ourselves of our pernicious self-will and our temporal possessions, which threaten to ruin true life.

Acts
27:10–20

On this way we speak of, these things are not to be thrown away and lost but rather turned to good use, for they are all to be given to the poor and needy, and what is much more, to Jesus Christ the Lord, in order that they may bear fruit a hundredfold.

The story in Exodus about the food that fell from heaven points out how true equality and community are to take shape. He who gathered much had nothing left over; he who gathered little had no less than the rest. The man who hangs on to even a very small part of his self-will or his property as his own private possession is no different from or better than the very richest man. He is rich enough to be disobedient to the will of God.

These are the characteristics of the true people of God. Jesus loved to use sheep, doves, and vines as symbols because by nature none of these like to be alone; they always want to be together. However brightly a coal may glow, it will soon go out if it is left alone. Hence the importance of gathering. Those who had been called by Christ remained together after they had left their parents, their trades, their professions. That is what Jesus means by His parable of the great banquet and the wedding of the king's son, when the servants were sent to call all the people together. Why did his anger fall on those who had been invited first? Because they

John 10:1; 15:5

let their private, domestic concerns keep them away. Again and again we see that man with his present nature finds it very hard to practice true community; true community feeds the poor every day at breakfast, dinner, and the common supper table. Men hang on to property like caterpillars to a cabbage leaf. Self-will and selfishness constantly stand in the way! How many are hindered and held back by it! However wonderfully they may speak in several languages, they have no life because they have no love.

Where there is no community there is no true love. True love means growth for the whole organism, whose members are all interdependent and serve each other. That is the outward form of the inner working of the Spirit, the organism of the Body governed by Christ. We see the same thing among the bees, who all work with equal zeal gathering honey; none of them hold anything back for selfish needs. They fly hither and yon with the greatest zeal and live in community together. Not one of them keeps any property for itself.

If only we did not love our property and

our own will! If only we loved the life of poverty as Jesus showed it, if only we loved obedience to God as much as we love being rich and respected! If only everybody did not hang on to his own will! Then the truth of Christ's death would not appear as foolishness. Instead, it would be the power of God, which saves us.

1 Cor.
1:18

COMMUNITY IS NOT COMPULSORY

We can see many clear signs that show the way to true love and community. But it is quite wrong to accuse us of making life in community a matter of compulsion. By no means. It is Another who demands it and compels us to it; but neither He nor we want to force anyone. Never! Whoever is not driven by love and an inner calling should leave it alone. It is an urgent longing for enduring life and joy, it is fear of God's wrath, that drives us and urges us to obey Him. That is the source of community life. It is not we men. It is not our invention. It cannot be our undertaking. Many of us have had a livelihood and property and a strong self-will. We liked it

all, too. We felt comfortable in it. But love
for Christ and for the poor drove us to do
what we do and confess to now. It was the
recognition of God. So we found out the
truth of the saying, "If you want the one,
you must let the other go." We recognized
the truth that no one can obey two
masters. We cannot belong to God and
Mammon at the same time.

Matt.
6:24

Thus it is a decision of the will, not compulsion. Among the Jews it is left to the
guest to decide whether he will partake of
the Passover meal or not. He can take it or
leave it. Jesus points again and again to
man's will: "If anyone wants to follow me,
he must go the way of death." "If you
want life, you must keep the commandments." And the Lord let the unwilling
man go his own way.

Ex.
12:48

Matt.
16:24–26
Matt.
19:17

But Jesus wants more than our good
will. He wants us to have joy in it, the joy
of one who has lost something of little
value and found a priceless treasure, like
the man in the parable of the Kingdom
who, in pure joy and without any compulsion, sells all he has for the sake of this
new treasure. It means more to him than

Matt.
13:44

all the money, all the riches, and all the property in the world. Therefore we should not set store by what is petty and worthless, but give it up for the sake of the one and only treasure. That is the best exchange we can make in life. It is the source of permanent well-being, expressed in enduring life, enduring joy, and genuine happiness. Whoever does not want to act out of this good will, this deeply surrendered will, whoever does not want to act for the sake of God and the poor, should leave it alone.

Some people are not without light and recognition of the truth, yet they do not want to step completely into the light. They hinder others from seeing the full light because they still love wealth and its benefits. They have enough recognition to see that on the Day of reckoning, self-seeking will not be justified and praised. But to excuse themselves they claim that community living is an endless source of dissent and strife, as if Christ who is the Lord, the apostles, and the Holy Spirit did not know what they were doing when they brought community life into being. They may be taking certain unhappy marriages as a parallel; man and wife live together in disunity, and of them it is unfortunately said that they love each other best at a distance. But in a good marriage it is different. Each one bears with the weaknesses of the other. Both together bear joy and sorrow as they come.

How much more does that apply to the new life of community, in which a whole people of God should bear with one another in love and forgive each other everything! They make allowances for each other. They can never forsake each other because of human weakness. They do not desert each other. We know very well that Jesus turned sharply on Peter. We know of disputes among the first disciples. Did they therefore desert one another? Could the unity of the Spirit be lost on this account? Or shall the communal life of Christ and His apostles be despised or rejected on this account? That is impossible. Now we can understand why Christ, who is our Lord, insists so much upon reconciliation and forgiveness.

1 Cor. 7
Eph. 5

Matt.
16:23
John 13

Matt.
5:21–26

Even at the time of the early Christians there was plenty of unpleasantness among the believers. Was the unity of the Spirit lost because of that? The Church remained united in spite of it, that one Church to which we must listen if we do not want to be outside. It would be wonderful if a people of God could live in uninterrupted peace, completely without blemish or defilement or any hateful thing. But because of our human weakness, such disturbances happen all the time. One ought never, on account of such shortcomings and weaknesses, to reject a whole people. "Don't throw the baby out with the bath water."

These things will not be an obstacle to anyone who is intent on building up Church community for the sake of love and salvation. He will be filled with a Rom. 12 burning zeal to build up a living organism and to make the sacrifices demanded by the Spirit. That includes the surrender of all his possessions and all his strength in true service to God. He surrenders his whole self. That is how he finds true

Matt.
5:14,15

Gelassenheit.[1] If a light is to burn, it must consume itself. That is the only way it can give light.

Luke
18:22
Matt.
19:21

Acts 5

Now we understand why Christ who is the Lord became poor for our sakes. That is why He had to say, "Sell all you have, and give to the poor." So we can understand why Ananias, though he had kept back only a small part of his money to provide for the future, had to meet death along with his wife in such a terrible way.

Luke
3:11

It is a question of what a man does or has done to the least of his fellowmen. John the Baptist, the forerunner of Jesus, had already said, "Whoever has two jackets should give to him who has none. And he who has food should do likewise." Whoever speaks of Christ and of love and yet refuses to hand his property over to the community for the sake of Christ and the poor proves by his actions that he loves

---

[1] *Gelassenheit* has no equivalent in one word in English. Its meaning includes the grateful acceptance of whatever God gives, even suffering and death, the forsaking of all self-will, all selfishness, and all concern for private property.

the things of this world more than Christ.
Blessed are the poor who have given their Matt. 5
goods for the sake of the poor. It must be
done for the sake of the poor.

But it is even more important that on
this way we surrender ourselves and
become inwardly free and recollected,
gratefully accepting all God sends. For
then there will be nothing to which our
hearts cling more firmly than to our
brothers in the faith, the members of the
common life. The emphatic words of Jesus Matt. 6:19
not to gather belongings on earth can
never be reconciled with the holding of
private property.

Instead of looking after our own 1 Cor. 10:24
interests we must look after the needs of
others. Love does not seek its own advantage. Again and again the question of self-
seeking comes up. Everyone must seek
with such constant zeal to serve the common need that he produces, if possible, a
hundredfold profit. He who has worked
faithfully in this way with his modest
strength will be entrusted with great
responsibility. What he has worked at will
never leave him. Such work cannot be in

vain, for it is the work of love in the service of those who are consecrated to God.

Phil.
2:4 Time and again we are enjoined to further the common interest in every way possible. As the old saying goes: Self-interest is bad interest; self-will belongs in Hell.

THE IMPOSSIBLE BECOMES POSSIBLE

Many thousands regard it as impossible to surrender all property and self-will. But Christ knew that it was possible. He stood before God. He could demand it. Historic examples stand as mighty proof that this Gen. 12 way is actually feasible. Abraham showed it to be feasible when he left his rich homeland. And Moses was able to leave his comfortable court life. So we should not be surprised that it was possible for Matt.
4:18–22 apostles of Jesus Christ to leave family and work, boat and net, in fact everything Phil.
3:4–11 they had. Quite unexpectedly, even Paul was enabled to throw away high rank, personal greatness and prestige, as if they were dirt. For Christ himself had proved Luke
9:58 something a thousand times greater. He had left the greatest to become poorer than animals in their holes and birds in their nests. These have their own place of rest. He had none. He opened up the new way on which He held all things in common with His disciples, in shared poverty. *One* kept the purse for *all*. And furthermore, as Jesus had foretold, the Spirit of unity came with such power over this company that suddenly thousands found the will to community, in the face of which they could no longer be concerned about their former possessions. They adopted just that attitude which so many now look upon as impossible.

Acts 2:41–47

From then on in the course of the centuries there were many thousands who gave up completely not only a considerable fortune, but what is more, their self-will. Many of them came with empty hands to the Church they had been searching for; for the rest of their lives they were thankful for it. And in this way many, very many, have come to us (the Hutterian Brothers), partly from other Brotherhoods, particularly those in Switzerland. Some of these had already been proclaiming the truth they had recognized, often at the risk of their lives; they brought many others with them. Most of them bore testimony to the Word to the end of their lives. The Church sent them out time after time into different countries. Often they had to pay for it with their lives. They were threatened with death by fire, water, and the sword. To the end, they testified courageously to the truth. So this way of community has actually been put into practice. As we can see in the early Church, which held to community of goods, this way has proved to be good and from God.

COMMUNITY IS SYMBOLIZED IN THE LORD'S SUPPER

To this first Church, the Lord's Supper was given as a uniting and sharing in *one* loaf and *one* body. The grain had to die for the sake of the unity of the loaf. Only by dying was it able to take root and grow in the field and withstand all the storms. Only in this way could it bear fruit. Similarly, each individual must give

Matt.
10:39

himself up, must die to himself, if he wants
to follow Christ on His way. Then in turn
the harvested grain had to be crushed and
milled if it was to become bread. Our own
will undergoes the same for the sake of
community. It must be broken if we are to   1 Cor. 9
belong to the community of the Supper
and to serve in communal work. Furthermore, the grains had to be brought
together into *one* flour and *one* loaf. Not
one grain could preserve itself as it was or
keep what it had. No kernel could remain
isolated. Every grain had given itself and
its whole strength into the bread.

In the same way, the grapes have to be
pressed for the wine. Every grape gives all
its strength and all its juice into the one
wine. In it no grape can stay as it is. This is
the only way wine can be made. Grapes or
kernels that remain whole are only fit for
pigs or the manure heap. They are far
from being bread and wine. In keeping
their own strength and individuality they
lose everything and remain lost.

Here we see the most powerful picture
of community. That is how Christ pre-
sented it to those who were with Him at

the Supper. But even this uniform loaf is broken, just as Christ let His Body be broken. For us this means that the stubbornness of self-will is broken and that we must be ready to suffer and die, even in community. God himself brings this about by letting His power break in upon us, and that is what we pray for. His power streams out over us as love, as the love that brings all God's truth to fulfillment.

John 13:34,35

As Christ has loved us, so love reigns among us. By this His flock will be known. This is the the only way we can hold the Lord's Supper and community of the table. Everything we were or had, all strength and energy and property were given for common use. Like the loaf and the wine, we have become one. Whoever wants to be a brother, whoever has a longing to share in the breaking of the bread and in prayer, cannot reject community.

Matt. 6:9–13

We never ask in the Lord's Prayer for *my* bread or *thy* bread. We ask for *our* bread, *our* daily bread, the opposite of private

John 6:5–14

property. Each time Christ distributed bread, He gave to many, to all, to each alike, no matter how small the supply was.

He did not want to give to any one person
alone. So the small became great, the little
became much.

COMMUNITY IS THE FULFILLMENT
OF LOVE

Talk of faith and brotherliness does not
go together with wearing expensive
clothes, dining well every day, or piling up
riches. The man who saves and
accumulates always does it for himself and
his family. Whether he lives or dies, his
brothers and sisters in the faith have little
or nothing to expect from him. How can
he speak of love to God, of love to his
neighbor, when the desire for wealth is
doing its destructive work in him?

When we are filled with the spirit of
community, we become simple and
modest. We will be satisfied with what
little food and clothing we have. On other
points, people who honestly call
themselves brothers can easily find a common recognition and reach a common
agreement in faith; for example that it is
God's will to shun war and weapons once

Luke
12:16,
22–31

1 Tim.
6:6–8

Isa. 2:4

and for all. But about possessions, in spite of the prophets and apostles, men will fight and struggle against the clear truth. Any profits from our work should not be hoarded. The fruits of our work must be put at the disposal of all our brothers in God. They are for the feeding, housing, and clothing of the poor, the hungry, and the old. It was through love that Jesus became poor and one of the lowliest on earth.

John
15:9,10
So He commands us as our Lord to love one another in the same way He loved us. That means that we make our fellow citizens in His Kingdom fellow heirs of all our goods, that we accept one another as members of the Household of God, that we close neither our hearts nor our purses to any need of a brother. Then, and then only, will God's love remain with us. That alone is genuine love. Ungenuine love is no love. Genuine love prompts us to give all our goods—and even our bodies—with an undivided heart. That is the way to the light. That is community. Where there is no genuine love, there is no faith.

1 John
3:11–18

Our love for our fellowmen must be so great that it compels us to share all our possessions with them; anyone who does not have that love for his neighbor should not think that the blood of Christ frees him from sin. As love springs from faith, so works spring from love. The only true "charity," consisting in acts of fervent love, is inseparable from true life and real freedom from sin. Active love will urge us to work for the overcoming of need and poverty rather than for our own benefit. Whoever does otherwise has not a spark or drop of divine love. He who loves God must love all men who have their life from God. If we really believe that all men have one God and one Father, we cannot possibly seek to gain or maintain an advantage over one of our brothers. If we still seek our own advantage, then love is extinguished and cold in us. We see the need and poverty of His children; we could help, but we do not do it, perhaps even saying, "Should I give bread to people I do not know?" So we become evil. We want to keep for ourselves what has been stolen from others. We are pleased we have

1 Cor.
13:3

1 Pet.
4:8
Hebr.
13:16

1 Sam.
25:11

1 Sam.
30:21–25

succeeded in life. Those who have dropped behind on the way get nothing from us. Do *they* not need their share just as we do? This is how we lose our feeling for justice. It grows darker and darker around us because we cannot love our brother. The cries of the poor surround us like dark shadows; they have nothing and suffer privation while we have more than enough of the best.

Matt.
18:7
Luke
6:24–26
1 Cor.
11:17–34

That is a public scandal. The cries of "Woe!" uttered by Jesus surround us. How hard the Apostle Paul had to struggle in his day for the new order! Even among the Christians there were poor people who went hungry while others had plenty. Let us never forget that *nothing* can stand before God except love. That was the Gospel from the beginning. That is the source of the rich and unfailing strength that enables us to follow the com-

1 John
3:16

mand to give up our possessions and our very lives for the sake of the brothers.

We should not think that we are sacrificing our lives only when we face the sword or some other violent death. No. We have to give up our lives in good times too. When we are achieving something and things are going well, we should give our lives to serve our neighbors. Just at such times we are expected to give up everything and not spare ourselves. Paul could have done many things, but he wanted only what was for the good of all. So it is a question of wanting the good for others instead of for oneself. Therefore I will even give up my own judgment, poor or good, if it causes a brother to fall. We forfeit the love of God if we cling to our possessions in the face of our brother's need. For we should love, not with words, but with deeds and in truth. The love that works through us must be the same as that love in which God gave His Son.

1 Cor.
10:23,24

1 John
3:18

THE VISION OF THE KINGDOM

The way of love for our neighbor is the way Jesus leads us into the realm of His lordship, into His Kingdom. In comparison, everything else is dirt and rubbish. Joy-filled life streams out from this new City, from this radiant City-Church. If in the face of this world of the future a

Rev.
21;22

Luke
12:20

man still longs for the pleasures of the senses and for possessions, he is a fool. His present life will soon be demanded of him. Then his heirs will quarrel over his estate. The worms have long been waiting for his body. It is simply stupid not to be able to let go of one's worthless possessions in order to gain the coming Fatherland—just as stupid as refusing to exchange a worthless grain of corn for a diamond, or a poor clay pitcher for a golden dish. The only wise thing is free surrender, holding on to nothing. The only great thing is the faithfulness that makes a man hand in all his goods. This faithfulness is what God expects of every man without exception. It applies to rich and poor alike. He who is faithful in this radical sense with his few possessions will be entrusted with the stewardship of great things. He will judge and rule over the whole world and all its spirits. Such great things God has in store for insignificant men, if they will only love.

In the face of the shining lordship of God, one's immediate needs become extremely unimportant. They matter next to nothing. One cannot hold on to property when one stands before God. Between members of His Kingdom, companions in the faith, there is an end of mine and thine. We bear with joy the loss of our possessions (worthless, however precious they seem) as soon as we discover the greater good. This is enduring and gives no cause for fear. It gives courage. He who lives in faith enters that wonderful land of God's rulership. Then his thoughts are no longer with his coffers. They are where Christ is ruling with God. Therefore it is never enough to shun the revolting sins. Self-will—not the most obvious and despicable sins—is what prevents people from accepting the invitation to the wedding feast and the banquet. A man stays away for the sake of his own field, his own responsibilities, his own yoke of oxen, his own wife, his own business. It is merely the natural self-interest needed for daily subsistence that causes men to ignore the fellowship of the common meal. Time and again this is what makes us unworthy of the invitation—the invitation given to all.

Matt. 22;25
Luke 14:16–24

The fig tree was not cursed on account

Matt. 21:19

of bad or poisonous fruit. It was condemned to wither away because it could
have borne good fruit and did not do so.
Out of repentance and turning around
must come good fruit. A new life that does
not produce good fruit is not genuine. The
Baptist tells us what this good fruit is: giving away your second coat and feeding
those in need. Faith is power, the power
that gives strength to bear fruit. Then we
will provide food and drink and clothing,
and our labor as well, for those who need
it; then we will put love for the brothers
and for all men into practice; and then, if
we are consistent in this service, we will
become simple and modest in our own
needs. This surrender will not let us
become lazy or unfruitful. That is the fruit
that God demands; that is the fruitfulness
brought about by brotherly love, the living
sap of the new tree. In such a life, God and
the brothers and sisters become greater
than everything else. Whoever is not ready
for this remains blind and unpurified. All
talk of Christ remains aimless talk and idle
opinion as long as our thoughts and
longings are concerned with personal aims

Luke
3:11

2 Peter
1:8

arising from our worldly condition. Only faith that brings forth love opens the door to that other Kingdom in which Jesus is Ruler. Jesus, our Healer and Savior, leads the way into this new life and Kingdom.

COMMUNITY IS THE TRUE FASTING AND SACRIFICE

Everything that was said about almsgiving and fasting in the Old Covenant (and also valued in the New Covenant) is fulfilled in such a life. It is a matter of depriving ourselves in order to give bread to the hungry, shelter to the homeless, and clothing and bedding to those who are cold. When we do these services, light and health enter our house and our life. Then there is nothing we need in the whole world, for our thoughts are filled with God and His Kingdom. It is not in the fasting or the sacrifice itself that we meet God. In fasting as in sacrifice, it is not the cult or the solemn ceremony that moves Him. He does not want them. What He does want and demand is what is good: justice, love, and good deeds. There is a thirst for the

Micah
6:6–8

living God at work in all these things, pointing to the salvation and healing which is in Jesus Christ. Then the heavens are rent. Then comes the One who was to come. The people of old saw His coming from afar. The old man Simeon held the Child in his arms, and we seek Him with joy and with all our heart as the great gift that can come from God alone.

Luke
2:25–32

God created man to walk erect with his head up. Man is not meant to be like the animals that hang their heads earthward. He is not meant to be preoccupied, like them, with the search for food. He belongs to the whole of God's cause and to the Kingdom.

The believing man steps into a new life. He is asleep or even dead to his previous life. All desires that are directed toward the earth are killed. Love for property and attachment to possessions have died with them. The vice of avarice hangs like a leaden weight on a man, pulling him down. Once a man has died, he will no longer be found in his own house. Once a man is buried, he is no longer seen on his own land or in his favorite tavern. The man who has died has left behind his wealth and property. After death no man's wealth, house, money, or goods belong to him anymore. This is how we understand the truth that we must die to the present world. Having died, we are no longer found among our possessions. From the point of view of self-will and desire for possessions we are in fact no longer living. To walk with God means to sacrifice ourselves just as Christ did. To give body and life means much more, not less, than to leave goods and chattels. Out of this strength to die we maintain a new order in a united household. Like children who are equally loved by their parents, we live in community and share our food and all our goods. We have left our previous way of life behind us just as though we had died.

GREED IS ONE OF THE WORST EVILS

Whatever separates us from the Kingdom of God, whatever has no part in His realm, is vice and must be publicly condemned. In God's eyes, greed in any

1 Cor. 5:9–11
Gal. 5:19–21

form belongs together with fornication and all other impurity. But very few realize that the apostles were right in their judgment, putting the two things on one level—love of money and immorality; to the apostles, both are guilt and sin, poison and weeds. But because most men cling to them with might and main, they are blind to this truth. With the rich that is obvious. The poor merely lack the means and opportunity to do the same. In their hearts they are just like the rich. We must not be deceived, however loudly they decry the avarice of the rich; they themselves are no better. Many of them boast that they are not miserly, whereas they are full of the devil of drinking and the demon of extravagance. Their drunken breath gives proof of their insane covetousness. They would love to have plenty of money in their pockets to satisfy their greed!

Passion for money is the root of all filth just as much for the miser as for the spendthrift. Those who love possessions should never forget that avarice is essentially nothing but idolatry. For men cling to money as they should cling to God.

Col.
3:5

They serve it as they should serve God. Their idols are silver and gold. No one who is in the service of idolatry, impure passion, or love of money can come close to the Kingdom of God. On these points, Christ the Lord is hard and inaccessible; His coming Kingdom is closed to them. The man who knows this gives his goods to the poor so that they may bear fruit a hundredfold; if he acts otherwise, everything will be taken from him.

Hos. 8:4

CHRIST WANTS THE POOR

The man who is settled in riches and property refuses the invitation to the Kingdom. He does not want to listen. He does not want to come. God calls the poor because the rich refuse. If the lords and nobles and business magnates refuse, the kingly joy of freedom and community is offered to the humble and enslaved. God gives it to the simplest of the simple. He would just as gladly give it to the high, the mighty, and the influential if only they would become simple enough to want to come. All should come. None are to be

Matt. 11:25
James 2:5

John 6:37
Titus 2:11

rejected. Healing and riches have come to all men and are available to everyone. That sounds agreeable to our ears; even so we do not want them because there is more involved, namely that in exchange for them we have to give up and leave everything that conflicts with the nature of God. Such is the covetous will of the present world that from the beginning it has caused us to struggle against recognizing the truth. "Is this voice really from God?" Great and clever people will not believe it. They push love away. God calls them repeatedly, wanting to gather them under the protecting strength of His love. He wants it. They do not. That is what Jesus said.

Matt.
23:37

They do not want to follow His call and influence. Thus they compel Him to use sharper weapons; He had to use the sharpest language in speaking to them. The poor listened to Him. Many of them went with Him. Rich and great men caused Him pain. So He had to cry out the threefold woe: woe because they are rich, woe because they are full and they laugh, woe because they are honored and pop-

Luke
6:24–26

ular. But still they are not excluded. Christ brings His atonement and reconciliation to the whole world. But it will be hard, very hard, for the rich to overcome themselves. It will be hard, very hard, for them to leave riches, property, and self-will. It will be hard, very hard, for them to learn obedience and live in community. It will be hard, very hard, for them to enter into the Kingdom of God.

What frightens them away is clear. The New Covenant does not promise good days, it does not lead us through rich lands. The history of the Old Covenant shows that whenever horses and chariots and silver and gold were piled up, the land was strewn with idols and sin. Again and again there arose prophets foretelling need and poverty and proclaiming the end of the corruption brought about in this way. Good days have never been good for men.

Therefore God established a New Covenant, a completely new one. But misery, despisal, the gallows, and poverty are so hard for us men to accept that we persist in thinking this new way is impossible. Therefore the Son had to be the first to

Isa. 2:7,8

tread this impossible way. Since then nobody could reject it as impossible, for it had been trodden. Since then we have had a Leader and Pioneer of the faith who, poor and despised, has trodden the way to the end. The end could not be anything but the extreme consequence of this way, execution as a criminal! Lazarus had to end his life in poverty and misery. Joseph and Job had to suffer bitter poverty. In the same way, the New Covenant demands that we remain firm to the end even in the most distressing need. And that is how we shall find great and exulting joy!

Hebr.
12:2,3

COMMUNITY IS NOT A SOFT WAY

Pampering oneself with fine clothing is out of the question. On this road one has to step into many a dirty puddle. Pampering and self-indulgence go hand in hand with possessions, riches, and sensuality. They do not belong to the way of poverty. This way leads to the cruel suffering of a bitter death. Opulence must be left to wealthy households and their vermin. Excess of any kind goes hand in hand with luxury and hypocrisy; excessive eating and drinking are forms of this same soft indulgence in nonessentials. We call it despicable weakness.

The austere life of John the Baptist, so poor in food and clothing, was there for all to see. That made it possible for him to demand that men share all their goods with their fellows, and to proclaim fire and destruction over all the unfruitful chaff. Let no one who wants to be known as a believer or a brother teach the broad way of covetous desires. Let us not entertain the delusion that it is not necessary to turn our backs on wealth and possessions, that it is not necessary to embark on community life in full surrender. It is abusing the Scripture in support of a teaching completely alien to it, to try to make the hard truth acceptable and comfortable for the rich; that is utterly impossible in fact. We need a strict impartiality in our vision. Only then are we able to recognize the way of truth, the clear leading of the divine Word. The whole of Scripture tells of what was revealed and brought to fulfillment by the Spirit in the first Church at Jerusalem.

Matt. 3:1–4

PRIVATE PROPERTY CANNOT BE
DEFENDED

The strong ruler Mammon opposes this
guidance of the Holy Spirit; he opposes
the clear promises of God, which carry
God's power within them; and he opposes
all those who follow this leading. Again
and again he employs lovers of property to
do his work of covering up and distorting
the truth. He gets them to use pious words
in support of their disorderly way of life
and their possession of money, but he
often makes mistakes in his choice of
words. He works against himself when he
makes them quote the case of the false
apostle Simon to support his arguments.
Like Judas Iscariot and Ananias and
Sapphira, Simon, with all his money, was
cursed. Certainly one can quote the Apostle Paul as calling the rich of this world to
give with glad hearts and use their money
rightly. Certainly one can emphasize that
John the Baptist to begin with spoke only
of the first step in the new life, that is,
doing no man violence or injustice. Certainly Paul bade carnal men who were still

Acts
8:18–23

1 Tim.
6:17,18

in the infant stage to put money aside for the Church at Jerusalem, which lived in community. These are examples of transitional stages, however, that were to be outgrown.

Instead of trying to provide a certain justification of private property by these pious arguments, the rich should rather say quite openly that they choose to follow the way of the world. They want to follow it, even though property leads to servitude. They want to hold on to it, even though life in community would bring freedom and spiritual life. If they choose to hold on to their animal nature, let them keep their own hole or nest! Jesus at any rate quite clearly rejected property. Whoever walks with Him cannot keep anything of his own. Some people may argue that owning communal property is no different from owning private property. The answer is that what belongs to the community is neither mine nor thine. Common property excludes private property. Life in community means devoting one's life and strength to working for the benefit of all.

The door to this community life stands

wide open. Come out of your private nests! Out of your private houses! Stop looking after your own affairs! Away with self-will! Sell everything! Give to those who have nothing! Come! Come, follow Me! Renounce all you have, then you can be My disciple. Do you really want to follow Me? Then give up yourself. Leave your goods and chattels; let go of yourself. Follow Me. I have nothing of My own. I have not even a place to lie down and rest. Is it because of your field, or your work, or your household that you do not want to come? Are you holding on to such little things? Do you love your self-interest and possessions so much? Then, of course, you cannot sit at the table of My community. You do not belong to Me.

Matt.
19:21

This is how Christ speaks to those who are held back by the ideas that rule the whole world. Their lives will never be fruitful. To vindicate themselves they take counsel with the many others who, like them, hold on to their own nests and, like them, want very much to be Christians and still keep their possessions. They want

to uphold property, so they have to be-
little life to community. And they end up
by neglecting and despising the clear way
of Christ, His perfect order, and His very
truth and life. Then the Word, which had
already been at work in them, flees from
their hearts; their hearts are turned away
from faith. They return to seeking their
own food. They are unwilling to work
their fields and keep house for the common purse. They become like moles and
foxes that undermine the communal plan-
tations and cause them to depreciate. And
still some feel in their hearts that they cannot deny the existence of love when it cre-
ates a life in community that is there for
all to see. In the depths of their being
they recognize this fact as good and necessary, but the right moment, the favorable
opportunity, never seems to come. First
one thing stops them, then another. So the
structure of community that should serve
the House of the Lord never gets started.
But for continuing the old life in their pan-
eled houses, the right time always seems
to be there. (Haggai 1:4) The true reason

lies deep. What they love most is not God, but holding on to their things. They still have far to go.

LOVE'S REFINING FIRE

There are many who have given up this or that form of injustice but remain utterly involved in it in other respects. Of the ten virgins who went to meet the Bridegroom, five had to stay outside: the flames of their festive lamps were not burning. Their faithfulness was extinguished; it was not enough. Of the trusted servants whom the landlord put in charge of his property, one had to be sent away for the same reason— lack of faithfulness. In the flock of animals that are all considered clean, the goats will in the end be separated from the sheep.

The same separation takes place here on the way of surrender. The doors are open, people want to come in, but only faithfulness and truth count. Not pious words but willing deeds born of faith belong to the new Kingdom. People can talk about all kinds of wonderful forms of

Matt.
25:1–33

Isa.
26:2

Matt.
7:21

worship, but they are still on uncertain, slippery ground. They do not want the way of action and *Gelassenheit*. No one dares it. It demands too much. It demands unconditional faithfulness in giving up everything! Riches and a life of comfort are murderous, slippery ground, on which everything is bound to collapse.

The day of testing will come. Then everything will melt and break like ice. Then it will be evident what kind of life people have led. They did no good deed to Jesus, for they did not keep His Word and did not truly love Him. And therefore they could also not love those who belong to Him. In the face of this, it will be no use asking any questions or making any excuses. They are rejected. They recoiled from the supreme test of the refining fire. This fire could have proved in good time whether there was real gold in them or whether what looked like faith was only a delusion. Ecclus. 2:5

Gelassenheit is the name of the refining fire that gives the decisive answer to this question. In this heat, all dross and inferior metals are discarded. In it they are removed, disposed of, eliminated. What is

freed is the pure gold: faith, and the love
that comes from faith. What is left behind
is everything else that one had. God and
Mammon cannot remain amalgamated.
That is the test of faith which the rich
young man, Ananias and Sapphira, and
many thousands of others had to undergo.
This fiery test showed what meant most to
them: their pious self-will and their
possessions—or Christ in every fellow-
man! This furnace burns away everything
that blocks and hinders. It has the same
effect as the needle's eye or the narrow
gate. None of the things we have been
dragging along with us can get through.
Fire is needed if gold is to be proved.

Everyone has to go through this test! It
was so from the beginning. When the earth
was created, God saw that everything was
good in its own way. Only about man God
did not say that he was good. Instead, He
set him a test in order to see whether he
would be good or bad. In this test man
first showed what he was; he made the
wrong choice. Abraham too had to
undergo this test in its sharpest form. The
same thing happened to the Israelites, who

Gen.
2:16,17;
3:1–6

were called out to be a people in wealthy Egypt and then led into the desert. Poverty was their test, and the prohibition of certain meats was part of it. In the case of Job the nature of this test was even clearer. Job 1:9–12

Each time something becomes the object of man's greatest love, God steps in. Through Jesus, God strikes at that self-will and greed harder than ever before. Whoever goes through this trial and chooses the way of Jesus is given the greatest responsibility, entrusted to him after he has left house, family, and goods for Christ's sake. But whoever loves any of these things more than he loves Jesus does not belong to Jesus. Therefore love will decide, love born of faith; it is the refining fire of true *Gelassenheit*. What remains as purified gold is the love of God; it alone has a place in His Kingdom. Matt 10:37

God wants us to love the poor. Christian community is the best way to put this love into practice. Through hard and steady work, we can provide an adequate standard of living for the poor and homeless; we can provide food and spread the table for them at every mealtime. We can do this even while we own nothing ourselves. Through this service people are enabled to live who would otherwise have to beg from door to door or die of misery and starvation. This is done for love alone by all who live in community; purely for Christ's sake and the sake of the poor. It is

Gal.
6:10

a question of love and friendship and brotherhood; in the first place, love and friendship toward our brothers in the faith. Only in joyful dedication can this work be done.

Deut.
23:19,20

In such a life, there is no thought of income or profit; still less, interest and usury. They are out of the question. In the New Covenant, ownership, self-interest, and avarice are branded as injustice and wickedness. But stubborn self-will prevents men from recognizing their guilt in these sins, just as pride does. Avarice stands out so plainly that it is obvious to anyone; it makes one man rich and the other poor. One man could help the other but he does not do it. That is avarice. But there is another form of greed for money, which turns out to be just as avaricious:

the rich lend money at interest to their poorer brothers in the faith, in order to become a little richer. What about love and brotherhood? What about the conscience? How is anyone to recognize them as Christians? For surely the sign of discipleship is love.

JOHANN ARNDT AND MENNO SIMONS

Johann Arndt was a highly enlightened man, respected by his own people but despised by many others as a heretic.[1] He wrote much that was good and true about the Christian life. But he did not represent that the perfect word and highest command of love must be carried out in community and mutual help. He comes very close to the mark, for example, when he says of the apostles that they had to leave and disclaim everything they had, even their own self, before they could receive the Spirit from Above. He says that the true light was given to those who followed

[1] Johann Arndt, 1555–1621, German Lutheran churchman, author of devotional books widely used in Mennonite circles of that time.

Christ on this way. Johann Arndt saw that. If he had represented this direction truthfully instead of covering it up, he and his followers would have run into great danger. Never at any place or time could Church community flourish if its people represented the full light of the truth, for wherever a true spark of the light has tried to show itself, it has been attacked with persecution and annihilation. So the light of truth has always been squelched. People rushed at it with fire and sword whenever it tried to shine. They threatened to exterminate it with tyranny, torture, and execution. The nearer one gets to the truth, the more dangerous it becomes.

Even Menno Simons remained a little to one side of the truth. In his *Foundation* he testified earnestly and with enthusiasm to some essential points of Christian faith.[1] He came close, very close, to the truth about perfection. He condemned avarice, ostentation, arrogance, and the like in

[1] Menno Simons, 1496–1561. "Foundation of Christian Doctrine" (1539), pp. 105–226, *The Complete Writings of Menno Simons* (Scottdale, PA: Herald Press, 1956).

strong words. But he never spoke out clearly about the decisive choice placed before the rich young man or about the powerful creation of the early Church in Jerusalem, although he knew the Church had its origin in nothing less than the mighty inspiration of the Holy Spirit. In the early Church, the giving up of possessions and the holding of all goods in common were very clearly witnessed to, particularly in the case of Ananias and Sapphira.

Menno's writings seem to point very forcefully in this direction. He lashes out at lust for money and the increasing of the rich man's fortune. He does not mince his words in exposing the cruelty with which they oppress the poor and leave them in their misery. He uses very sharp words against the whole wide world and its scandalous profits. But in singling out the people of the world, the clergy, and the monks for these pointed attacks, he lulls to sleep his own brothers in the faith. Many of them were living in the same wealthy ostentation and lack of discipline. Some oppressed their poorer fellow believers instead of really helping them. The *Foundation* points particularly to those Mennonites who are proud of this writing by Menno Simons and who console the rich among them with it. Had Menno Simons demanded the fruits of life that are truly in keeping with love, he would surely have found fewer people to go with him. There have always been only a few who have really dared to take the narrow path.

TRUE COMMUNITY IS GOD'S WORK

In the recent and dangerous Reformation times, men of faith appeared again at last. They knew the Scriptures and were conversant with languages. The light was lit in them. They came forward. They testified sincerely to the truth. They offered to hold debates with learned people, for they were ready to have a member torn from their body for every false conviction that could be proved against them.

They set about God's work with power from on High. In the strength of God's almighty power, they took it up earnestly and vigorously. God's power is stronger than words can express. They fought their fight steadfastly and gallantly, even unto death, for they wore the right armor for this fight, and they had received the golden sword. Without yielding, they stood firmly in faith in Jesus Christ. Many of them forfeited goods and property, even their bodies and their lives. The banner of the great Sovereign Jesus Christ, the banner of blood and strife, went ahead of them. They followed it. His royal highway was their road.

We should follow their faith, for they prepared the way. They dared to undertake their unique work in the strength of the almighty God. They did it for the sake of community as the fruits of perfect love. They began it for the sake of the community of all believers. They defended it against the yawning abyss and the raging depths. They carried it through against all the doubts of those who said it was impossible. And they gave it a perfect Order in accordance with Christ's will.

In spite of persecution, the work grew. At various times we had twenty and more

households or Bruderhofs. These were
situated in different places, market towns,
and villages. Sometimes there would be
from three to four hundred people living
together in one household, and even as
many as six hundred. These hundreds of
people had a common kitchen, bakery,
and dining room, a common school, a
common maternity house and baby
nursery. In each household there was
only one steward or householder. With
the money brought in by the various
workshops and other sources of income,
he bought whatever was needed: grain,
wine, wool, hemp, salt, cattle, and so on.
To everyone in the house, children and
adults, the steward gave according to each
one's need. Special food was fetched
for school and preschool children, for
mothers of newborn babies up to the age
of six weeks, and for any others who
needed it. Everybody else went to the dining room for the common meal. Certain
sisters were asked to look after the sick,
bringing them their meals and nursing
them. The elderly sat separately at table
and were offered a little more than the

young and healthy. To each was given according to his need, as far as possible.

The communities established according to this Order have continued uninterruptedly for well over a hundred years [as of 1650]. Only by the grace of God was this possible. It was not easy. We have gone through very hard times. We have often been thrown into dire poverty through plundering and burning. We have suffered much damage through the great wars.[1] Several households were completely annihilated and lost everything. But each time we moved together again. Time after time another suitable place was found to take in all those who had been persecuted and driven out. We have borne with one another and suffered together in great poverty as well as we were able.

There were also better times when things went well. But in those very bad times we had to use up everything that belonged to the Church. Everything that had been set aside during the good times had to be used up. We could well have

---

[1] The religious wars of the sixteenth and seventeenth centuries, also the Thirty Years' War (1618–1648).

used a thousand times over the great amount of goods that was stolen from us by Francis Cardinal von Dietrichstein. It was not surplus but the result of genuine brotherly responsibility to care for the needs of the whole Church. In this spirit, time and again we met the need with whatever we had left after being driven out of house and home in times of persecution. This happened repeatedly for the sake of our faith in Christ Jesus. Time and again we had to set out on our wanderings with the many little children and the many sick. At those times particularly we held together. How could we possibly abandon the weak and old in such need! We cared for them to the best of our ability and did all we possibly could for them. We looked after one another as brothers and sisters should. And God was standing by our side. That alone enabled us to stand our ground. That alone enabled us to grow.

Many sincere men, women, and young people came to us, having left well-to-do homes or big farms and, above all, their own strong self-will and in some cases high public standing. Some came to us from other Brotherhoods. Unto death, they witnessed to the divine truth of community as an absolute necessity. We need not be surprised that in the face of such remarkable facts there was much lying and slander. It was the same with Christ and the apostles. So it will remain until the end of the world.

Matt. 5:11,12
Luke 6:22,23

PRIVATE PROPERTY BECOMES CHURCH PROPERTY

To establish community life takes all our strength. It is nothing less than *the* cause, the cause of Him who is our Lord. We should count the cost beforehand!

It ought not to happen (as it did a number of times) that people come in a quick blaze of enthusiasm, wanting to take part, but their will proves to be insufficiently grounded and cannot carry them through. In the long run they find it hard to submit to the Orders that arise inevitably from the Spirit of Christ. Sooner or later their courage and zeal flag. They break their covenant. They leave the path. They quarrel and give trouble. The difficulties are greatest with those who fall away after having given in their property, originally with good intentions. And now they demand it back. They want it again for themselves.

That is why we do not right away accept a final surrender of property from one who wants to begin a life of brotherhood with us. He is given enough time to learn what our convictions are and what message we proclaim, and to find out what our way of living and working together means for him. To begin with, we put aside what he brings with him into the community, either to be returned to him eventually or used for the common cause. If later on the community life no longer appeals to him, he can go his way. Then we are glad to give him back what had belonged to him, to the last penny. He is at liberty to go where he sees the best opportunities for himself.

If after this time of testing he recognizes the truth, if he has really experienced the truth and asks for baptism of his own free will, he becomes a part of community life. Whatever he has brought with him is now laid before him. Whether little or much, it is given back to him. Now he can hand it over to the Church, for that is as it should be. Now it is accepted. Now the poor and needy can benefit from it. It will be used wherever it is needed.

But should it ever happen that he becomes unfaithful and in contradiction to his clear commitment demands to have his previous belongings back, nothing can be given back to him. After all, he did not hand it in so that it might later be given back to him! Before God and in all justice we owe him nothing. We treated him in the way we have just described. What a man gives up in the morning is no longer his in the afternoon. Therefore whenever a person is received into membership, all this is said to him. Certainly, as things are at the moment this is hardly necessary. People are so very poor that we have to give all those who come to us everything they need, from the very first day on.

Much evil is said about us on this point. Although this just conduct is valid before God and required of all believers, many people (even among the Swiss Brethren) condemn it. The only arguments they can bring up are false ones. On the Day of the Lord, when His judgment comes, all lovers of property will have to recognize the truth. Then they will recognize wealth for the murderous weed that it is. Then they will see that it choked the living seed within them, so that they were unable to bear fruit in life.

ORDER AND OBEDIENCE

The deepest root of this noxious weed is certainly not the external and tangible aspect of property. It is rather the arbitrary self-will and obstinacy anchored in the willful heart, the will of the ego, which is directed against the communal will. Whoever is accepted into our communal life has to be obedient in every aspect of his life. It is not only a matter of a man leaving his goods and chattels. It goes deeper than that: through obedience he enters into discipleship. In obedience he has to subordinate himself to the Church. He has to be willing to be used by the Church in whatever work and service is considered right and useful. If we first sur- _{2 Cor.} render to Christ himself as our Lord, we ^{8:5} submit to the will of God. With this, we have in fact given ourselves to the Church and to the brothers and sisters. This is confirmed by the New Testament. It _{Rom.} means real sacrifice, the surrender of our ^{12:1} lives.

Christ the Lord himself expected the same of His apostles and disciples. He demanded obedience of them. Wherever He sent them they went, even if it cost _{Matt.} them their lives. He sent them like ^{10:16–20} defenseless creatures into the midst of beasts of prey. They were expected to be submissive and obedient to men insofar as these were given authority by Him. He who listens to the apostles listens to Jesus, _{Luke} and therefore to God, from whom Jesus ^{10:16} has His mission. The prophets foretell that from all the wildernesses of this world men who are like wild beasts will become capable of living together in community, that people who are like wolves will become like lambs, that a little child will _{Isa.} be able to lead them all. ^{11:6}

For that to happen, obedience and a

definite order must be established. Otherwise people cannot live together as a people of God. So the apostles tell us to obey those who have been given authority. We have to subordinate ourselves to them because they have to give an account for our lives. Whoever looks down on them despises God himself! For He has given His Spirit into them. When Moses called together the people known as the company of Korah, they declared, "We will not come." And this disobedience was their downfall. The Apostle Paul emphasizes most strongly, "Have nothing to do with him who does not want to obey our words."

Further, the young should submit to the older ones. And more than that. Each one, yes, each one, should submit to the other. More significant still is the reason for this command: God sets His face against those who think highly of themselves; those who are aware of their own smallness and count themselves among the lowly will be rewarded by God. In the Old Covenant this attitude led to the harsh words, "Whoever rebels against your command-

Heb. 13:7

Num. 16:1–14

2 Thess. 3:14

1 Pet. 5:5

Josh. 1:16–18
Deut. 17:12

ment and disobeys your words, whatever
you command him, shall be put to death."
All believers must be led to joyful sub-
missiveness. It is in this submission that we
break with the Devil and our self-will.
"You no longer belong to yourselves." 1 Cor.
Nobody belongs to himself. He must do 6:19
whatever he is appointed to do by men
whom God calls. The Apostle Paul expects this obedience even in his absence.
He claims God as his authority for this.
Through Paul, God works on men to will Phil.
and to work. It is God who brings about 2:13
both the willing and the accomplishing of
good. Obedience and enthusiasm born of
the Spirit are constantly needed in God's
Household. Everyone does joyfully and
with a will what he is asked to do. He hates
and turns away from his own will.

Obedience takes the place of ritual
sacrifices. Disobedience is disbelief and
arises out of it. Disobedience is demonic 1 Sam.
sorcery, nothing but the selfish ends of 15:22,23
man's own will. Invocations to God and
the accompanying rituals strengthen man's
obstinate self-will to the point where disobedience becomes idolatry and sorcery of

the worst kind. Therefore any man who ignores as unnecessary, thus repudiating, the command of obedience given by God and Christ, has good cause to fear the Day of Judgment.

DISCIPLINE AND PURIFICATION

The bond of love is kept pure and intact by the correction of the Holy Spirit. People who are burdened with vices that spread and corrupt can have no part in it. This harmonious fellowship excludes any who are not part of the unanimous spirit. Man is by nature inclined to sin. In order to keep a people of God pure, it is very necessary that strict order and discipline are used in the right measure. Evil has to be warded off. The coarser vices and sins have to be publicly unmasked before all members of the community. This is the only way to awaken men's sense of shame about the worst sins and to sharpen their consciences. If a man hardens himself in rebellion, the extreme step of separation is unavoidable. Otherwise the whole community would be dragged into his sin and

1 Tim.
5:20

become party to it. If a curse lies on a community, the curse must be lifted. Otherwise God's Spirit cannot be with us, for He does not share His rulership with other spirits. The Apostle Paul therefore says, "Drive out the wicked person from among you." Deut. 17:7 1 Cor. 5:13

The Church should not be negligent in carrying out this Order. The way the world administers justice by capital punishment is the opposite from ours; instead we use the discipline of the Church. In the case of minor transgressions, this discipline consists of simple brotherly admonition. If anyone has acted wrongly toward another but has not committed a gross sin, a rebuke and warning is enough. But if a brother or a sister obstinately resists brotherly correction and helpful advice, then even these relatively small things have to be brought openly before the Church. If that brother is ready to listen to the Church and allow himself to be set straight, the right way to deal with the situation will be shown. Everything will be cleared up. But if he persists in his stubbornness and refuses to listen even to the Matt. 18:15–18

Church, then there is only one answer in this situation, and that is to cut him off and exclude him. It is better for someone with a heart full of poison to be cut off than for the entire Church to be brought into confusion or blemished.

The whole aim of this order of discipline, however, is not exclusion but a change of heart. It is not applied for a brother's ruin, even when he has fallen into flagrant sin, into besmirching sins of impurity, which make him deeply guilty before God. For the sake of example and warning, the truth must in this case be declared openly and brought to light before the Church. Even then such a brother should hold on to his hope and his faith. He should not go away and leave everything but should accept and bear what is put upon him by the Church. He should earnestly repent, no matter how many tears it may cost him or how much suffering it may involve. At the right time, when he is repentant, those who are united in the Church pray for him, and all of Heaven rejoices with them. After he has

Ps. 38

Luke
15:3–10

shown genuine repentance, he is received back with great joy in a meeting of the whole Church. They unanimously intercede for him that his sins need never be thought of again but are forgiven and removed forever. Christ gave His apostles authority and power to do this. What they bind is bound and what they loose is loosed. Christ gave them His breath and said, "Receive the Holy Spirit. If you forgive the sins of any, they are forgiven; if you retain the sins of any, they are retained." (John 20:22–23) For all those who abandon their evil ways that means a tremendous joy, a joy that leads to life. Each one who makes this covenant with us, each one who becomes a part of our life together, promises to do and take upon himself all that has been said here. He promises to accept brotherly admonition and discipline for himself at any time. He promises that he for his part will also make use of brotherly warning and discipline whenever it is called for.[1]

Matt. 16:19

---

[1]The present editors took the liberty of transposing to the end a brief section about mission that followed here in the original text.

OUR CHILDREN

For all these things, separation from the world is necessary. That applies in a particular way to the education of our children, which concerns us greatly because it is a most important matter. We must constantly endeavor to find the best ways of bringing up our children. Not only in the later teens but even from earliest childhood, what is corrupt in human nature begins to stir. From an early age it threatens to grow. We can compare it to iron that tends to rust, or soil which by its very nature encourages weeds to grow. Only with constant effort can they both be kept clean. It is a fact that from early childhood the children of men love all kinds of evil. They have within them a covetous will and a tendency to selfish desires. That makes itself felt most strongly if children are exposed daily to bad and corrupting examples. With their natural instinct to imitate they will follow these examples. Then the desire to keep on imitating what they see grows in them until we become helpless in the face of their evil doings. If we try to combat the evil, they will do what they want to do secretly as long as they are exposed to such bad influences.

Added to this is the fact that many parents are by nature soft with their own children. They have not the strength to fight seriously against what is wrong in them. Therefore there is double cause, indeed thousandfold cause, to seek Christian community for the sake of the children, so that they can be kept clearly separate from the world. The value of such separation is that children can be prevented from falling into godless ways and bringing shame to their parents, who are otherwise good and honest people. The burden of children's disgrace falls on the parents, for it is they who should have brought up their children properly. If children fall into evil ways, into pride and arrogance, drunkenness, loose living, or other wickedness, as long as these children live it will be said of the parents that they brought up their children to their own dishonor and shame. They neglected discipline. This bad reputation will follow father and mother to the grave. Long after they are gone, the wrong upbringing of their children will be on people's lips. God 1 Sam. 2 himself sees it in the same way. He let the whole house of Eli be destroyed because Eli, though blameless in his own life, had neglected to discipline his sons. The heaviest burden is the fate of the children who are going to ruin, for their life and blood are on our heads. The right education and upbringing of children, as we try to practice it in our households, proves to be absolutely neccesary.

The guidance of young people is threatened by yet another danger, arising out of poverty. Many who know the good way and try to follow it give their own flesh and blood into the service of men who have no faith. It even happens that children are allowed to work in taverns and inns. Children are the highest and most precious treasure, the noblest and best of all that is entrusted to us. We must look after them with holy zeal. On the great Day of the Lord we will have to account for what has become of them.

That applies also to those who are ambitious for their children. They hand them over to the world so that they will get to know the things that are important in the world. As a result, many such children have turned away from the faith of their parents. The salvation of these young people is taken so lightly, so little value is set on it, that these defenseless young people are handed over to beasts of prey. They are practically pushed toward their ruin. They are delivered to the worst and most godless influences, which in the end must spell their ruin. Who can answer for that before God? The Holy Scriptures and the voice of our own consciences could and should protect us from this. Menno Simons challenges us in his book *Foundation*: parents who live with God should rather see their children burned at the stake or brought into outward misfortune of the worst kind than let them be educated in the pomp and show of the world. If they get drawn into it or marry into it, they may sink into far worse destruction than poverty, sickness, and death can bring. All the saints call us to separate ourselves from the world. Far be it from us to get involved in the world or mix ourselves up in it. Therefore we confess openly that this calamity must be avoided with utmost determination, let men ridicule and slander us as much as they will! What should be taken more seriously than man's salvation and his eternal life?

In the clear light of God's order it is a dirty stain, a serious fault, when marriage is permitted between a believer and an unbeliever. From such a marriage evil of all kinds arises, and sorrow, pain, confusion, disorder, and apostasy. Such a marriage is contrary to God's definite command. "You shall not give your daughters to their sons, nor take their daughters for your sons." "If you marry among alien peoples, you will go to ruin." Ezra ordered all alien women and children, all alien sons and daughters, to be sent away.

In this as in all other questions we are all too ready to make empty, highflown excuses. Certainly a couple already

Deut. 7:3

Josh. 23:12,13

Ezra 10
1 Esdras 9

1 Cor. 7:13–15

married should not be separated if the partners are able to live together without harm to their faith. But the Apostle Paul never said that a believer and an unbeliever should take one another in marriage. Such mixed marriages never lead to happiness. God always hated them. Therefore, if elders of Christian circles permit them, theirs will not be a pure, unblemished Church. Christ did not even permit a man to go to bury his father or take leave of his former companions. How much less, then, would He have permitted a union that has such grave consequences. It is disorder! For instance, it may lead to inheritances being withheld from the poor on the death of the parents. Quarrels about such inheritances usually end up to the advantage of the unbelievers. That should not happen. No one should give away his father's inheritance.

Eph. 5:27

Num. 36:3,4

This makes it obvious that when love is too weak it leads in a wrong direction; then there is no community, no order, and no true obedience anymore. Everyone does as he wants, particularly with his property. We are reminded of the saying:

"If you slip on the top step, you will fall down the whole flight of stairs."

From the Holy Scriptures you have gained a clear conception of true baptism and the Lord's Supper, of the great gift of redemption given by our Lord Jesus Christ. We are of one mind in this as is clearly expressed in the book of the Five Articles.[1] The spreading of the Gospel is very close to our hearts. Before the war and the hard times it brought, we devoted much of our strength to the mission task. The command of Christ and the tireless way the apostles carried it out has urged us each year to send messengers out both near and far. They were to reach out to those who were full of glowing zeal and to gather for God all those who belong to Him. The Lord himself sent out His twelve apostles to spread the truth. He also sent out the seventy, always two by two. There is much work to do. The harvest is great. Pray the Lord of the harvest to send out His laborers. It is His last command that

Luke
10:1,2

Matt.
9:37,38

[1]See footnote 1, p. 2.

His disciples should go out. "Go into the whole world and preach the joyful news to the whole creation. He who believes and is baptized will be saved." (Mark 16:15–16)

We have no doubt about the whole basis of our faith. It is in our conduct in daily life that we feel very imperfect. But also in these things we strive with all our strength to reach the goal. Our hearts and minds are fully assured about the foundation and the truth of God's light and our perception of it. In all humility we are certain that what we teach is the true content of the Scripture, nay, its very foundation, and Jesus Christ is its cornerstone. We know that no one can lay any other foundation. There is but one, and that is Jesus Christ. And no matter how many enemies rise up with great power and might, the Lamb shall overcome—Babel will fall.

Phil.
3:12–14

1 Cor.
3:11

ICH WEISS EIN LAND

Ich weiß ein Land in naher Fern, es liegt in leerer Flur.
Die Wüste sperrt des Berges Kern, dort sucht man Goldes Spur.
Der reichste Schatz der weiten Erd gehört dem Einheits-Mut.
Gold-Ader-Tiefen nie erhört verschenken edles Gut.

Der Weg, den dieses Land dir weist, ist frei nur dem, der frei—
Der frei von aller Habe reist, ließ alles, was es sei!
Das eigne Gut im alten Land, er gab's der Armen Not.
Der Wille riß das eigne Band, er tat's um Christi Tod.

Von drüben winkt das neue Reich. Die Freude wartet sein.
Sie bricht das Alte hart und gleich, sie tötet Mein and Dein.
Es bleibt der größte Tor der Erd, wer hängt am eignen Gut.
Er tappt in Blindheit unerhört, stürzt tot in eigne Glut.

Im Tode bleibt er fern dem Land, wo Freudeneinheit strahlt.
Zu lange blieb ihm unerkannt, daß Geiz nur Tod bezahlt.
Drum Brüder, auf zur Bruderschaft! Gemeinschaft leuchtet auf!
Die Habe sei hinweggerafft—geeint auf einen Hauf.

Wo keiner mehr im Eigennutz den eignen Reichtum sucht,
Wo Einheit wirkt in Geistesschutz, bleibt Eigentum verrucht.
Drum lassen wir das eigne Land, hebt hoch Gemeinschafts-Gut!
Wirkt, schafft und gebt mit fester Hand, heil jedem, der es tut!

Eberhard Arnold, Rhön Bruderhof, 1928

I KNOW A LAND

I know a land, not far away, midst country bare and cold.
The wilderness hems in its hills, where seekers dig for gold.
Earth's richest treasure comes to those with courage to unite.
Gold-veins of depths we never dreamed yield riches pure
   and bright.

The road to this new land is free for only him to find
Who travels free from all his goods, who left them all behind.
The goods he owned in his old land, he gave to those in need.
His will broke loose from selfish bonds—for Christ, who
   died and freed.

This Kingdom beckons us to come and share its childlike joys.
Joy shatters soon the time-worn ways, and 'yours' and 'mine'
   destroys.
He is the greatest fool on earth who to his riches clings,
He gropes in blindness, black as night—and death of heart
   it brings.

In this he stands far from the Land of joyous unity.
That greed must lead to living death, too long he could not see.
So brothers, up to brotherhood, community's new day,
With all things common in one love—possessions swept away!

Where none his own possessions seeks nor his own gains to win,
Where fruits of unity are giv'n, there property is sin.
So let us leave our native land to share all things anew,
To work and give with willing hand! O happy those who do!

Translation

CLAUS FELBINGER

Confession of Faith
Addressed to the
Council of Landshut

1560

INTRODUCTION[1]

This confession of faith is both a great
Christian document and one most
characteristic for the spirit of Anabaptism
at its best. It was composed by Claus
Felbinger, a Hutterite brother and a
blacksmith by trade, who had been chosen
Servant of the Word by the Brotherhood
in Moravia in 1558. While not yet confirmed in this service he went on a missionary trip to Bavaria in 1560, together
with another brother, Hans Leutner. In
the week before Easter 1560, the two
brothers were caught by the authorities,
like so many others before and after them,
and were put into prison. Here they were
interrogated, mainly on the issue of infant

[1]Slightly abridged and adapted from the article by
Robert Friedmann, "Claus Felbinger's Confession of
1560," *The Mennonite Quarterly Review*, April 1955,
pp. 141–144.

baptism, which was the most acute issue of all between the brothers and the authorities of State and Church. Then they were brought to the fortress of Landshut in Bavaria, where they were put into separate prison cells. Felbinger was even chained to his place. From then to July of that year, the authorities tried with all possible means to make them recant. They were interrogated and tortured, and then again drawn into disputations.

Felbinger remained steadfast and absolutely certain of his position. His was a genuine and well-founded faith, which he was able to present so skillfully that everyone was amazed, not expecting a humble blacksmith to know all the arguments so clearly. When at one point Felbinger said that he intended to stay in the "simplicity of Christ," the "chancellor" (apparently the interrogating State official) answered, "I do not think you are so simple.[1] I think there would not be one in a hundred who could give an account of

[1]Note the double meaning of the term "simplicity" (*Einfalt*), meaning both nonsophistication and poorness of mind.

himself as well as you do. Neither do I
consider you an 'enthusiast' (*Schwärmer*),
such as run around everywhere and have
no good foundations for their teachings."[1]

From prison Felbinger sent two epistles
home to the Brotherhood in Moravia.
(There were always humble men around
who were willing to carry such mail back
and forth, and there were always some
loopholes in the prison system that made it
possible to smuggle out these documents.)
In one of these epistles he gave a detailed
report of his imprisonment and of the
talks and disputations with the authorities.
From here the above-quoted remark was
later inserted in the Hutterian *Geschicht-
Buch.* Felbinger also submitted to the
authorities a written confession of faith or
Rechenschaft (in a new translation here), a
copy of which was sent home where it was
studied, copied, and spread among all the
brothers. But all Felbinger's "defense,"
that is, his explanation of why he became
an Anabaptist, why he went to Bavaria as

---

[1]Rudolf Wolkan, ed., *Geschicht-Buch der Hutterischen
Brüder*, published by the Hutterian Brethren in Canada
(Vienna, Carl Fromme G.m.b.H., 1923), p. 306.

a missionary, and why he had taken such a stand from which he was not willing to deviate, was in vain. Since he certainly was not minded to recant, he was condemned to die, together with his brother-companion. On July 19, 1560, at Landshut, both were beheaded. The chronicle describes the scene: while the other brother was being beheaded, "Claus looked on unafraid, with good fine color. If one were not informed one could have thought that he was not involved at all in this affair."[1]

The epistles and the *Rechenschaft* (confession or account, perhaps more correctly "testimony") now became a real message. In 1569, when another Hutterite brother, Veit Grünberger, was arrested and brought to Salzburg, where he lay in prison for seven years, he too was interrogated and involved in disputations with the clergy, which he promptly reported home to Moravia. We read: "They asked him for his confession of faith. Answer: 'Your lord, the prince [the Archbishop of Salzburg], has all the

[1]Wolkan, p. 307.

account of our religion he needs. I understand that the sheriff has sent our books [the famous Hutterite manuscript codices] to the governor. In them he may well find what we believe. For two of our ministers who were executed, Claus Felbinger at Landshut, and Hänsl Mändel at Innsbruck, have given a full account of our faith, and I would not know how to improve on that.'"[1]

The Anabaptist confessions of faith are not creedal statements in a narrow sense, binding for the Church, but are rather testimonies or personal statements, making clear how every brother understood personally the Anabaptist outlook, and how he would indicate his own position. These statements were Christian documents of a genuine character and of great spiritual depth, not something learned or repetitions of what others had said. Here a personal spiritual experience of rebirth and radical change in outlook on life and its values receive expression with an amazing immediacy and liveliness. One cannot help being impressed by this

[1]Wolkan, pp. 373–374, footnote.

matter-of-fact certitude about things spiritual and by the clarity as to why this way was chosen and how it must be pursued. There is no fear whatsoever of suffering and death, and with all the respect due to authorities, a courageous stand before judges and other officials becomes apparent. There is much nobility of mind, quite in contrast to the uncouthness of most officials and the times in general, a dignity which proves in itself that these people went through a real conversion. Although each brother defends himself independently and out of a personal commitment, Anabaptist documents by and large show an amazing likemindedness, proving again that whosoever was touched by the Spirit from on High experienced and understood the same truth. The world had no attraction for them, but also no dread anymore.

This document is no systematic or learned paper. It begins rather as a personal letter to the authorities showing them that they perhaps cannot understand the Anabaptists at all because of the unregenerate state of mind of the officials. But then Felbinger gradually turns to the different points of the interrogations and tries to explain the beliefs of the brothers in Moravia (and we may say of all Anabaptists). We do not have many documents of this kind of that time.[1] The meaning of baptism finds a beautiful interpretation: baptism is the acceptance of the new covenant with the Lord from which there is no way back. The Lord's Supper is understood as the ever renewed consecration of true Christian fellowship and brotherly unity. And toward the end of the document the great issue of sin is treated, above all the basic relationship between original sin and actual sin. This is perhaps the most important section of the document, in which Felbinger emphasizes the need for a distinction between "being born in sin" (which causes physical death for all men) and "committing sin" (which would cause eternal damnation). The Anabaptists believe that man can and must fight

[1]The foremost text is the well-known *Rechenschaft*, Peter Rideman, *Confession of Faith: Account of Our Religion, Doctrine, and Faith*, 2nd ed. (Rifton, NY: Plough Publishing House, 1970).

"the good fight" against sin—something which certainly was not the common belief of Christians of the sixteenth century, and which might not even be all too common today. In reply to the question, "Why Moravia?" that is, whether one could not be a good Christian anywhere, Claus Felbinger gives a very sensitive answer, allowing us an insight into the roots of the cohesiveness of genuine brotherhood as practiced among the Hutterites in Moravia. It is above all the motive of Christian brotherly love that shines through all these pages.

Although this document is of Hutterite origin, it yet may be considered as an expression of genuine Anabaptism in general. It is after all only one and the same idea which pervades it: true salvation can be found only in true discipleship; and this, in turn, is possible only through genuine rebirth and conversion of the heart.

April 1955   *Robert Friedmann*

CONFESSION OF FAITH

Dear lords and magistrates of this town of Landshut: God, who does nothing without a cause, has so disposed it that we two [Hans Leutner and myself[1]] have been arrested for the sake of divine truth and handed over to you as prisoners. The county sheriff in Neumarkt and his assistants have already questioned us twice about our way of life; and here in Landshut the governor's men have questioned us several times. But in my heart I feel I have not yet fully disclosed my mind in such a way that you may understand the basis of our faith.

It is therefore my earnest request that you take time and trouble to read this written confession of ours so that you may

[1]Wolkan, p. 304.

understand how we live and on what foundation we stand and build. In it you will see (if there is any divine spark in you) that we have done nothing hasty or unreasonable, although the world in its blindness calls us fools. We know God's Word cannot lie. When we build truly on the Word of God and our lives are in accordance with it, when we trust it, then our souls will suffer no harm and we will not allow the children of darkness to frighten us away from it. For this is the way we must enter the narrow gate. Few find it, but Christ has shown it to us as the way to life and has Himself gone this way before us. It leads through humiliation, suffering, pain, and fear; it is a narrow, slippery, rough, and hard path.

In this letter you will find most of the questions we have been asked and our answers, and with God's help we hope to stand firmly to them. We confess to this being God's truth, which indeed it is, and we trust in the Lord. Whatever He may allow you to inflict upon us will surely be for our good, for our salvation and comfort, since we love Him with heart and soul. And whatever you do to us will count heavily against you unless you change your lives and find true repentance.

SURRENDER TO GOD AND OBEDIENCE TO GOVERNMENT

First, my lords, you too are servants of God (though outside the perfection of Christ) because it is your task to punish evildoers and the wicked and to protect the devout. Therefore God has put the sword in your hands and granted you honor and dignity as long as obedience to you is justified. That is not against God. And we say to you: whoever disobeys the government in anything just and fair disobeys God's order; he is liable to punishment by the authorities, for it is their task to punish disobedience.

Therefore I urge you servants of God to consider your task. It is not that we are dismayed at the thought of having to suffer for our actions or our confession. Not in the least, for we do not feel worthy or able or good enough to suffer at all for the sake of God's Word. On the contrary, we praise God for having chosen us unworthy men to be true witnesses to His holy truth. That is what we promised in the covenant of true Christian baptism. We will lay down our lives if need be for the sake of His Name; we will not act willfully against God in either word or deed once we have recognized the truth, but with His help we will rather suffer death; we will walk according to His holy Word and adorn our faith with deeds pleasing to Him. For He has given us who believe in His Word grace and strength to do His will joyfully. This we were able to do only after we had surrendered our lives to Him completely, for He promised to give all true believers the strength to do what God demands of them and what is right in His sight. He promised to seal their faith with the power of the Holy Spirit. The Spirit will lead them into all truth and give assurance to their spirits so that they may know with certainty that they are God's children and fellow heirs of Christ, inasmuch as they have to suffer with Him.

John
16:13

Therefore, dear lords and servants of God, examine us as you will, you will not find that we have acted against God or offended any man. We live without doing harm to anyone, either here or elsewhere. But God's work is strange and wondrous to human eyes. His truth has always been unbearable and repugnant to the world. For all their wisdom, the wisest men on this earth have not been able to recognize Christ, who is eternal Truth. From the beginning, those born of the Spirit have had to suffer persecution at the hands of those born of the flesh, for the two have always hated each other. Christ himself has said of His wonderful coming into the world that He did not come to bring peace on earth but discord and the sword, dividing men two against three and three against two in such a way that they will find their greatest enemies within their own households. The Lord will bring it to pass that two will be in one bed, and one will be taken and the other left; two will be grinding at one mill, and one will be taken and the other left. What can be greater than to prepare the way by means of God's Word? Then God can call men by the Word of His grace. Then He can gather

Luke 12: 51–53; 17:34,35 Matt. 24:40

and set apart a holy people who will cherish and honor His covenant.

2 Thess.
3:2
So faith is not given to everybody. Some people accept Christ's teaching all of a piece. Others reject it as deception. Unless it is given to men from Above, unless it is revealed to them by the Father himself, they cannot grasp it. There is nothing we can do about that. We wish all men could grasp it and understand what they need for John
9:4 their salvation. They have to repent now in this time of grace, while it is still day. God's wrath hovers over the heads of the sinful and unrepentant; it will sweep all the godless into Hell. The unrighteous will not inherit God's Kingdom; it will be given to those who have cleansed their souls by obedience to God's truth and who patiently strive for eternal life by doing good deeds.

We have been asked why we came into this land [Bavaria], why we lead people astray. I answered that we have come not only into *this* land but into *every* land— wherever our language is known. God opens doors to us and shows us zealous hearts who truly seek Him, people who are dissatisfied with the ways of the world and are eager to do what is right; and to them we go, for it is God who sends us. Heaven and earth are the Lord's, and so are all men. We have given and sacrificed ourselves completely to Him. Wherever He sends us and wants to use us, there we will go in obedience to His divine will, regardless of what we may have to suffer.

Further we were asked: since the government is ordained by God and gets its power from Him and should therefore be feared and honored by everyone, why do you not do so?

Here is our answer: the government is not meant to be feared by the just but by the evildoers. It is meant as a shield for the just. That is why the Lord has put the sword in the hands of the government; He has ordained that taxes and duties be paid toward its yearly income so that the authorities can carry out their tasks and give the necessary protection. If they fail in their task, God will punish them all the more. So we are glad and willing to be subject to the government for the sake of the Lord, and we will not resist it in anything that is just and fair. But as soon as we are expected to do anything contrary to our faith and consciences, such as swearing oaths or paying war taxes or hangman's dues, we disregard the government's orders. This is not because of pride and obstinacy, but because we fear God alone. For we owe it to God to obey Him rather than men.

Acts
5:29

The reason why we fear God is this: Christ forbids the beloved ones whom He has prepared for eternal life to give way to human anger. He commands them not to take revenge and not to kill, but to leave vengeance in God's hands. That is why we cannot assist in the shedding of blood; for any Christian taught by God through His Son, it is wrong to do that. We should be children, free of vengeance and rancor, guileless as doves. To men of old it was rightly said,"You shall love your neighbor and hate your enemy." But Christ says, "Love your enemies and pray for those who persecute you, so that you may be sons of your Father who is in Heaven." We have to distinguish between the Old

Matt.
5:43–45

Testament and the New. "You have heard Matt. 5:38,39 that it was said, 'An eye for an eye and a tooth for a tooth,'"—a hand for a hand and a head for a head—"But I say to you, Do not resist one who is evil."

The fact that we do not swear oaths, or use the swearing of oaths the way the world does, has its origin in Christ's words: "Again you have heard that it was Matt. 5:33–37 said to the men of old, 'You shall not swear falsely, but shall perform to the Lord what you have sworn.' But I say to you, Do not swear at all, either by heaven, for it is the throne of God, or by the earth." "Let what you say be simply 'Yes' or 'No'; anything more than this comes from evil." And so, dear lords and magistrates, you should keep in mind that whenever we have opposed you in any way, it was not out of pride but only because we fear God, who is indeed to be feared. The apostles did not allow the Jews or any government authority to push them into doing anything contrary to what they knew was right before God. Rather, they laid down their lives.

And that I too hope to do, with God's help. I will not let anyone stop me from saying what is right before God. I will speak about what I have seen and heard and experienced in my heart through the renewal given me by the Holy Spirit; that is, about the resurrection of Christ Jesus, who has given us new life—us who are His followers, who believe in Him and honor His Name, who give ourselves wholly to Him and let Him do with us as He pleases.

We have to say freely and publicly that among you it is not God's work that has been established but the Devil's; your deeds bear witness to this. What the Devil has planted thrives and grows, and injustice is rampant; there is no way of checking your sin. The world has become a wilderness, sunken in sin, and knows little or nothing of God. And now the very teaching of the Gospel has become a new and heretical teaching, a deception in the eyes of the world. As soon as God raises up a messenger of salvation for men, one who proclaims to them the true Word of God and shows them the path of salvation, they refuse to believe him and think he is a

1 John
1:1

madman or a fool. Anyone filled with the Spirit is considered stupid or insane. That shows how deeply deluded they are in their wickedness. They are trampling their own salvation underfoot and making themselves unworthy of eternal life. They do not believe that a man can serve God in true piety, without sin, because they believe it impossible to leave the Devil's sinful, godless ways.

If that were true, it would mean that Satan is stronger than God. That can never be! For Christ was sent into this world by His Father to destroy the power of the Devil, crush the head of the old Serpent, destroy his works, and take away sin. Take it away, that is, from all those who gladly want to have their sin taken away; those who listen to His holy Word, who believe it sincerely and keep it in a pure, good, and sensitive heart.

1 John 3:8

Does Christ make people accept His teaching by threatening them with prison and torture, as many do who are called Christians? O no! He speaks to those who thirst for His righteousness, who have ears to hear, whose hearts are heavy, who want to be freed of their sins—those who are called and urged by God.

NOT WORLDLY WISDOM BUT FAITH

In truth, faith is not for everyone. It is a gift, given to those who love God. God will not force anyone to serve Him. He loves free and willing hearts who serve Him with gladness of soul and joyfully do what is right. For it is written: those who believe will obey God out of love. And again: those who fear God will seek to please Him and keep His commandments. For the Spirit promised by God to those who believe in Him is not a timid and slavish one, but a childlike, enthusiastic, free, and willing Spirit, through whom we cry to God the Father with faith and trust. He is our powerful Advocate before God. John has said, "We have confidence before God; and we receive from him whatever we ask, because we keep his commandments and do what pleases him."

How then can the world, that is, all the wanton sinners and the unjust, all those who allow themselves to be ruled by evil

Deut.
10:12–14;
11:1
1 John
5:2

2 Tim.
1:7

1 John
3:21,22

and driven from one evil deed to another—how can they call upon God in that confidence? They not only break God's commandments, but everything they do is repugnant to God; they abuse His holy Name and anger His countenance. How shall He be gracious to them, even though they ask? The man born blind, whom Christ healed, said rightly, "We know that God does not listen to sinners, but if anyone is a worshiper of God and does his will, God listens to him." David said, "If I had cherished iniquity in my heart, the Lord would not have listened." And Christ said, "The true worshipers will worship the Father in spirit and truth, for such the Father seeks to worship him." We can see this also in the fact that Christ taught the Lord's Prayer not to unrepentant sinners but to His obedient children, to those who remained faithful to Him in all temptations and whom He cleansed for the sake of His Word. A willful sinner—one who is not surrendered to God in obedience— cannot truthfully pray the Lord's Prayer. If he does, he will be lying from the first

John
9:31

Ps.
66:18

John
4:23

word on; he will be mocking God and rousing His wrath and bringing vengeance on himself. Whatever is not based on faith is sin. "To the corrupt and unbelieving nothing is pure; their very minds and consciences are corrupted"; but "to the pure all things are pure." The pure man's prayer is pleasing to God, for it is God's Spirit who urges him to it. Those who do not have God's Spirit are not God's children. Only those who are urged by the Spirit are His children.

Titus
1:15

How incredulous are the wise of this world when they are shown the narrow path! The teaching of Christ's Cross can be nothing but folly in the eyes of the lost. They claim that we are much too ambitious; that Christ has paid our debt and has done enough for us; that all a man needs to do is to believe this firmly and admit that he is a sinner, for God is merciful. Not a word about true repentance and new birth, without which there is no blessedness. True repentance means sinning no more, beginning a new and holy life with God, and breaking with the world.

The wise of this world flaunt their knowledge and say, "We find it in the Old and New Testament. In our opinion you are aiming much too high. If only those were to be saved who act as you do, the whole world would have to be damned." But we believe God's Word without any question. His Word is established and cannot lie. His Word does not conform to the world; rather, we men have to conform to the Word of God. The wise of this world think that because they have studied the Books and are well versed in them they lack nothing. That applies especially to the monks, clerics, and scribes. The foolish men! The wisdom of God cannot be gleaned from books or learned at the university; far from it. "For the fear of the Lord is the beginning of wisdom; and a good understanding have all those who practice it." Ps. 111:10

So we see that the mystery of the heavenly Kingdom is revealed only to those who faithfully follow Christ; the others have eyes and do not see, they have

Ps.
25:14

ears and do not hear. David says that the
secrets of God belong to those who fear
Him, and He makes known to them His

John
8:32

covenant. Those who remain true to
Christ's teaching will understand the
truth, and the truth will make them free.
Knowledge makes people puffed up, but
love heals and builds up. The worldly-wise
are repelled by the teaching of Christ's
Cross. Common sense warns us not to
come under the yoke, for our flesh rebels
against God.

1 Cor.
1:26–29

That is why Paul says, "Consider your
call, brethren; not many of you were wise
according to worldly standards, not many
were powerful, not many were of noble
birth; but God chose what is foolish in the
world to shame the wise ... so that no
human being might boast in the presence
of God," but all honor might be God's.
Christ praises His Father for having
hidden the truth from the mighty of this
world and revealed it to babes.

We are accused, further, of condemning
those who do not believe or act as we do.
That we deny. We condemn no one, but

we show men their damnable lives and warn them of damnation strictly according to the Lord's Word, which cannot lie. We believe that it will come to pass as His Word says, and for the sake of our loyalty to God's Word many of us are forced to lay down our lives. No man can condemn another. Judgment is in the hands of the Lord. But a man's evil, sinful deeds condemn him unless he breaks with them and shows honest fruits of repentance according to God's command.

BAPTISM

Another question I was asked had to do with baptism: how many times I had been baptized. I answered, once, as God has commanded. They asked me if I had not also been baptized by the brothers? I told them that the devout brothers who baptized me according to Christ's command did so after having taught me repentance and faith in the name of Jesus Christ; they baptized me on the confession of my faith according to my desire. And God, who is true to His promise, sealed my faith and strengthened it through the Holy Spirit, who has to this day protected me on the way of truth. Thus I hope to God that He will not take His Spirit from me until the end of my days.

Ps.
51:11

But I have no use for infant baptism. It is invented by men for the sake of money; the parsons use it to enrich themselves. It is a plant which the heavenly Father has not planted; therefore it must be rooted out. There is not one word either in the Old Testament or the New Testament to show that infant baptism was taught by Christ or practiced by His disciples. They had one and only one baptism; it was for those who were old enough to understand and accept the faith, who were awakened by the preaching of God's Word and themselves asked to enter God's covenant and become part of it. Through the covenant of true Christian baptism they broke with the sinful pleasures of this world and renounced the service of the Devil.

That is why the Devil does all he can through his messengers to prevent true Christian baptism from being revealed and why the Antichrist—that abomination of

Dan.
11:31;
12:11
Matt.
24:15

desolation, the Pope—makes so much of infant baptism.[1] That accursed practice was invented only to insult true Christian baptism as Christ commands it and to stop people from fully surrendering to God.

Baptism is the covenant of a good conscience with God and a public declaration that the baptized believer has been accepted to "share in the inheritance of the saints in light." What does a little child know of the covenant of a good conscience with God? That is all stuff and nonsense. Someone else takes the child's place, the godfather, who is expected to believe for him and does not know himself what faith is. He may be a drunkard, a blasphemer, an adulterer—a child of perdition. In short, it is absurd, a hoax. All kinds of evil, infamous people boast of the name "Christian," and the precious name becomes a cover-up for their wickedness.

1 Pet. 3:21

Col. 1:12

[1]Antichrist: a term used by the reformers, including Luther, who maintained that if the Pope claims that he represents Christ and at the same time accepts worldly dominion, he is the opposite of Christ, namely the ruler of this world, the Antichrist.

Moreover, the papacy and the clergy had by that time a long and well-known record of corruption.

What makes a man a Christian is not his baptism but his way of life. A Christian is one who lives a Christian life; if he lives a heathen life, he is a heathen. But the Antichrist has turned everything upside down and defends it with the sword: whoever will not believe him must die. And the priests of Baal cry out, "Beware! It is a time of great danger! The wolves are breaking in among the sheep!" How blind they are! So they have sheep? It has come to the point where the "sheep" tear the "wolves" and their "shepherds" want to shear them and suck their blood. They think their shepherds are messengers, whereas they can see by their very lives that they are not ruled by God's Spirit but by the spirit of wickedness. Can anyone who is evil speak of what is good? God will never entrust His holy Word to such blasphemers, for God is Himself the Word, and He entrusts it to those who are faithful.

1 Tim. 3:1–13
Tit. 3:1–11 The Apostle Paul wrote clearly in his Letters to Timothy and to Titus that a Christian must live a well-ordered life. He must be above reproach, the husband of

one wife, courageous, temperate, sensible, hospitable, an apt teacher of the faith, not addicted to much wine, not quarrelsome or slanderous, not greedy for gain, not violent but gentle. He must manage his own household well, helping his children to be God-fearing and respectful in every way. He must be well thought of by outsiders. He must be brave, not double-tongued, but sober, just, and holy, and carry with a good conscience the mysteries of faith.

Put your clergy in front of a mirror and ask yourselves whether any of these virtues are reflected in it. Does it not reflect rather the opposite? That is why their teaching does not change anyone; it bears no fruit. They do not speak God's truth, but only voice their own opinions out of the deceit of their hearts. The result is that they destroy themselves and corrupt those who listen to them, preventing no one from doing evil. Their words have no power to free anyone from sin or change anyone's life. They remain the same old sinful wineskins, unfit to hold the sweet wine of divine truth. The Holy Spirit refuses to dwell in anyone who is a slave of sin; He will have nothing to do with wicked hearts. So they are the blind leading the blind.

THE LORD'S SUPPER

I was also asked our opinion of the holy sacrament. I told them that the sacrament of the clergy is meaningless to me. Their blessing is a curse in God's eyes, for they despise His Word. But the Lord's Supper, Christ's Meal of Remembrance, means a great deal to me if it is held in a worthy and reverent manner. And that is no small matter.

So they asked me if I did not believe that Christ is present in the Meal with His blood and body, just as He suffered for us on the Cross. I said no. Christ has ascended to Heaven, where He sits at the right hand of God our heavenly Father. He will not let Himself be conjured down from Heaven into the hands of sinners so that they may then sell Him for money. He is the enemy of all evildoers; no one guilty of such madness can appear before His eyes. (See note on page 133.) Isa. 28:7

But, they say, He has clearly said, "This is my body and my blood." Yes, indeed, thanks be to God, we know how to interpret this sublime mystery, which He unveiled to His loved ones at that comforting Supper. With the bread and the wine He pointed to the community of His Body. Just as natural bread is made up of many grains ground by the millstones, giving all they have to each other and having community among themselves to form one loaf, and just as wine is made from many grapes that have given up their juice in the winepress to be gathered in one drink, so we ourselves have become one in Christ, living and dying with Him to become like Him. He is the Vine and we are His branches; He is the Head and we are His members. Matt. 26:26–28 Mark 14:22–24 Luke 22:19,20

But the branches must bear no other fruit than that which is in keeping with the nature of the Vine. All unfruitful branches will be cut off and thrown into the fire. The same is true of the members of Christ's Body: they should not grasp for earthly goods or entertain anything but that which Christ the Head directs them to and kindles in them through His Spirit. Those who do not have His Spirit are not His. But those who have given themselves wholly to God with heart and soul and all the members of their bodies, those who let The Holy Spirit rule them and teach them the truth, who surrender to the Lord in true *Gelassenheit*, who let God do His work in them and keep His Word in hearts that are pure—those are the ones who will bring forth good fruit in patience. Only these, in whose hearts the Word of God dwells—the Word that is life and Spirit (the flesh is of no use)—will eat Christ's body and drink His blood.

James 5:7

Whoever thinks he can do it any other way deceives himself. No sinner who has failed to obey the Spirit of truth and cleanse his heart so as to live in genuine brotherly love is allowed to share in this Meal. Christ celebrated it with His disciples, with those whom He declared pure by His Word in which they had believed. We should remember that Judas sat down at the table with an impure and superficial heart, scorning the Lord's injunction to consider every spoken word carefully—he did not take this to heart. Jesus even referred to him when He said that one of their company was a traitor. These words shocked all the others even though they were innocent. But the heart of Judas was hardened through sin and lying, so that he was unable to hear the Word. And what happened when Judas took the morsel? Satan entered into him and drove him to fulfill his own judgment. Judas was bound to sin against his Master and become an instrument of His innocent death, a warning to all who would sit at the Lord's Table with unprepared, unrepentant, impure, and sinful hearts; they are hypocrites, only pretending to be true members of Christ's Body and totally surrendered to Him.

Yes, indeed, the Lord knows each one of them. There is no deceiving Him! A man who dares to defy or tempt God only harms himself. In his Letter to the Corinthians, the Apostle Paul gives a very serious warning to everyone to examine himself before partaking of the Lord's

Matt. 12:36

John 12:37–30

1 Cor. 11:27–32

Supper as to whether he is pure of heart, obedient to God, and a true member of His Body. If he is not, he should stay away from it. For if he eats and drinks and is not cleansed, he becomes guilty of the body and blood of the Lord; he eats judgment upon himself, for he does not discern the Body, and people cannot tell what kind of members belong to the Body of Christ. Christ does not want impure, illegitimate members who still cling to themselves and others in creaturely love. No, He wants pure, holy members, just as He, the Lord, is holy—members who love God above all and cling to Him alone.

GOD'S PEOPLE ON EARTH

I was asked further why I separated myself from the holy Christian Church and joined a sect that is tolerated nowhere and obnoxious to emperor, king, princes, and indeed to all the world. I told them that I did not separate myself from the true Christian Church; on the contrary, I only really joined the Church by entering into the true community of saints through true Christian baptism. There is no doubt in my mind that this is where we find forgiveness and remission of sins, where we find the power given by the Holy Spirit to loose and to bind so that this will be valid both on earth and in Heaven. I know in my heart that no other teaching could have helped me to find true inner peace with God. For as soon as I heard God's voice in my heart and obediently answered, "Here I am," my soul was restored, and now I wait in hope and joy and quiet confidence for His salvation. Matt. 16:19; 18:18

Praise and thanks be to God for the love and compassion He has shown me, His unworthy servant. I am certain that God has removed my sins from me farther than night is removed from day. He will no longer remember my sins or hold them against me if from now on I walk faithfully in His sight. He has promised to remit all my sins and blot them out in the innocence of Christ Jesus. Of that I am certain. Jer. 31:34 Isa. 43:25

Could I ever have found such faith and certainty in God through my blind, unconscious infant baptism? It follows that I did not leave the true Christian

Church but separated myself from the so-
called Christian fellowship of sinners and
evildoers, fornicators, adulterers, gam-
blers, blasphemers, gluttons, drunkards,
liars, misers, and idolaters, who will not
cease to arouse God's wrath. All these I
left behind for good, and I want to have no
community with them either here or in the
Beyond, unless they in turn leave behind
their godless ways, recognize their sins,
and find true repentance.

God still has a devout people on this
earth, who have been shocked and star-
tled out of sin through His living Word. He
has called them out from the world and
gathered them to His Name through the
Holy Spirit. He has chosen them to be His
own, to praise His glory, to walk in His
ways, and to proclaim His power and
goodness. They shall adorn their faith
with works pleasing to Him, put on the
garment of innocence and the cloak of
righteousness, and wear at all times the
breastplate of upright deeds. Thus all we
teach and undertake remains in God so
that people may have an example of
godliness and be encouraged to examine

Eph.
6:14
1 Thess.
5:8

their own lives, to leave their godlessness
and turn from their sins to God. The Lord _{Acts 14:17} Acts 14:17
has never left Himself without a witness,
either in word or deed, so that no one may _{Rom. 1:20} Rom. 1:20
be able to make excuses for himself.

They say we are a sect that is obnoxious
to princes and lords and all the world, and
that everybody objects to us. That cannot
intimidate me or any true lover of God; it
strengthens our certainty and deepens our
faith in the proofs of God's working
wherever word and deed go hand in hand.
When Simeon held the little Baby Jesus in Luke 2:25–35
his arms in the Temple, he foretold to His
mother Mary that He would be the light of
the world and the salvation of all peoples
to the ends of the earth; and His sign will
be that men will reject Him. That means
not only Him but all those who follow
Him, who believe in Him and walk in His
footsteps. Jesus himself said, "If they have Matt. 10:25
called the master of the house Beelzebul,
how much more will they malign those of
his household." They will slander your
name and persecute you for the sake of the
Son of Man. "Blessed are you when men Matt. 5:11,12
revile you and persecute you and utter all

kinds of evil against you falsely on my account. Rejoice and be glad, for your reward is great in heaven, for so men persecuted the prophets who were before you."

Because they know nothing about God, they say, "Why don't you stay here? Is it impossible to do good and be saved right here? Or is salvation to be found only in Moravia?" Here is the answer: it is not at all impossible to do good and be saved right here, *if only people lived accordingly*! But they don't, and what is more, they prevent those who would like to and drive them to idolatry with threats of prison, torture, and the loss of their property. "Indeed all who desire to live a godly life in Christ Jesus will be persecuted," writes the Apostle Paul to Timothy.

2 Tim. 3:12

A devout heart that fears God cannot remain silent but must speak up and protest the wicked ways of those who do not please God, much less find salvation. That arouses their hatred, and the cry goes up: Away with the scoundrels! They think they are better than we are! They have no right to live! And so the godly have to flee Gen. 27:43 as Jacob, whom God loved, fled from the wicked Esau and his children to Mesopotamia [Haran] to stay with his relatives and fellow believers.

It is clear that salvation cannot be confined to a certain place or country, for God's Word will not be confined. Anyone who fears God and does what is right pleases God, wherever he may be. But all true children of God will work zealously together, not each on his own, and so they support and comfort each other. Nowhere is a sincere believer happier than in the presence of his brothers and fellow believers. They show each other love, reverence, and faithfulness and do good to each other. It is the divine nature of love that makes us feel we are in our neighbor's debt and urges us to serve him joyfully wherever we can. Brothers and sisters refresh each other by sharing the gifts God put into their hearts for the good of the Body of Christ, His holy Church, which is the gathering of all the believers who have made a common bond in God's love.

We have many examples of holy and devout men who have gone before us. Their words and deeds are a challenge for us to become like them. What can be a greater joy to the man who loves God! To the listening ear, wisdom is a precious jewel. And that was also the longing of David, who said in his Psalms, "Behold, how good and pleasant it is when brothers dwell in unity! It is like the precious oil upon the head, running down upon the beard of Aaron, running down on the collar of his robes! . . . For there the Lord has commanded the blessing, life for evermore." And again, "I do not sit with false men, nor do I consort with dissemblers; I hate the company of evildoers, and I will not sit with the wicked. I wash my hands in innocence, and go about thy altar, O Lord, singing aloud a song of thanksgiving, and telling all thy wondrous deeds. O Lord, I love the habitation of thy house, and the place where thy glory dwells." "Blessed are those who dwell in thy house, ever singing thy praise!"

In God's House the believers sing one song after another. Each brother and sister

Prov. 20:15

Ps. 133

Ps. 26:4–8

Ps. 84:4

is a challenge to the others to love God, to practice love, and to do good. For it is written, "With the loyal thou dost show thyself loyal; with the blameless man thou dost show thyself blameless; with the pure thou dost show thyself pure, and with the crooked thou dost show thyself perverse." And Sirach says, "Birds of a feather roost together." That is true of man, too; he seeks the company of his own kind. And woe betide the man who is alone when he falls. Who is going to help him to his feet?

2 Sam. 22:26,27
Ps. 18:25,26

Ecclus. 27:9

But community, perfect unity, and separation from the world are to be found only in the perfect Kingdom of Christ. We know that Christ has called out all those whom He appointed to have eternal life. With His death He sealed the New Covenant given by God in His mercy and won from His Father the promised Spirit, who shall lead all true believers into the truth. It is this Spirit who taught them the way of community, of which we read in the first five chapters of the Acts of the Apostles: all who believed were together and had all things in common; and no one said that any of the things he possessed was his

Acts 2,3,5

own. Those who possessed land or houses sold them and brought the proceeds and laid them at the apostles' feet; and distribution was made to each as any had need. And there was not a needy person among them. And they devoted themselves to the apostles' teaching and fellowship, to the breaking of bread and to prayer. And they were one heart and one soul, and none of the rest dared join them.

And God still has such a Church on earth, the gathering of those who live and work in true community, sharing all blessings of the Spirit and all temporal goods. God wants His children to be like Him, not false but ruled by His Holy Spirit, who gathered them and therefore keeps them as one. I can testify that this is true of the brothers and sisters.

ORIGINAL SIN AND THE SINNER

We are being accused of justifying ourselves. They say, "None is just but God alone; we will wait with the avowed sinner in the Temple till God justifies us." Well and good! If only they came to the true

Temple where there is remission of sins! This Temple is the true Christian Church, the community of saints. But as they refuse to enter it, how can God justify them in it? We, however, came to this Temple and confessed ourselves to be sinners before God and His Holy Spirit. The earnest prayer of the devout justified us and freed us from our sins, for which we praise God. With His help we want to hold on to His justification, just like the avowed sinner in the Temple, and sin no more so that nothing worse may befall us. You do not even understand that passage, for you are like the Pharisee who wanted to please God without repenting. You let yourselves go and sin against God's mercy; you do not even want to leave behind your disgraceful ways, your sins and wickedness, so that God can put new life into your hearts. If, as you claim, Christ freed you from sin, why do you still *act* in such a godless way? You are just as free as a prisoner who, while his hands and feet are in the stocks, claims he is free; he would rightly be laughed at by everyone. No one who sins is free. He is a slave of sin, and

John
5:14

Luke
18:11

John
8:34–36

the slave will not be an heir: that is only for the Son and those whom the Son of God makes truly free.

Now they argue: "I don't believe that a man can serve God without sin, for sin is always with us." That is true, but there is a big difference between *being sinful* and *committing sin*. No man born of woman and of the seed of man is without sin. We all share in the original sin that comes to us from Adam. Sin has come down through all of mankind; as David said, "I was brought forth in iniquity, and in sin did my mother conceive me." The Book of Genesis says, "The imagination of man's heart is evil from his youth." And John: "If we say we have no sin, we deceive ourselves, and the truth is not in us." And James: "Desire when it has conceived gives birth to sin; and sin when it is full-grown brings forth death." From all of this it is clear how deep the damage of original sin is in man; in fact it is the cause of man's earthly death.

We can see in little children that they have no awareness of sin and have never committed any. They have never provoked

Ps.
51:5

Gen.
8:21

John
1:8

James
1:15

God's wrath. And still they have to die to their own nature in their way, just as much as we grown-ups; but sin does not harm their souls. As a child grows, his inclination to sin increases. Once a child has grown up and reached the age of understanding, it will become clear which way he is going, but until then he must be taught in the fear of God and led to the Lord Jesus and trained with the rod, which helps to keep naughtiness out of his heart. If he has pleasure in godly things, believes and loves God's Word, and longs to enter into the covenant with all of God's children to live a devout life until his end, and if he is given a good witness and has proved himself, he will be baptized according to his wish and on the confession of his faith, in the name of the Father, the Son, and the Holy Spirit. But if he refuses to let himself be guided by God's Word and live accordingly, and commits sin and evil deeds, he will be sent away from the Church because no warning or discipline helps him. That is how we bring up our children.

I have already said that there is a lot of talk about sin without making any distinction, as though the Apostles Paul, John, or James were men who sinned, since they admitted that they were not without sin. We must keep in mind that original sin, the urges of the sinful flesh, human desire and lust, evil notions and sinful thoughts—all the various ways a man is tempted to do wrong—tempt the believer as much as anyone. He is not free of these temptations; they are all sin. Sin rises up in his members, and it fills him with fear and trembling because he loves God. He would give anything to get rid of it. It appalls him and troubles his heart; it makes him sad, and he cries to God, begging Him to take it away, for surely God delights in true godliness. That is what the Apostle Paul did. He wrote, "A thorn was given me in the flesh, a messenger of Satan, to harass me, to keep me from being too elated. Three times I besought the Lord about this, that it should leave me; but he said to me, 'My grace is sufficient for you, for my power is made perfect in weakness.'" And

2 Cor. 12:7,8

in another place: "I delight in the law of God, in my inmost self, but I see in my members another law at war with the law of my mind and making me captive to the law of sin which dwells in my members. Wretched man that I am! Who will deliver me from this body of death?" "But thanks be to God, who gives us the victory through our Lord Jesus Christ." _{Rom. 7:22–24} _{1 Cor. 15:57}

In the same way, many godly men have deplored and bewailed that "law of sin" to the end of their lives. Still, they were not sinners anymore after their conversion, once they were granted forgiveness. Paul writes to the Galatians, "If, in our endeavor to be justified in Christ, we ourselves were found to be sinners, is Christ then an agent of sin?" Are we to have nothing but sin from Him? Certainly not! How could we who have died to sin still live sinful lives? But the world calls everyone a sinner in whom there is sin, without distinction. Even in a little child there is sin, but he is not a sinner. The same is true of anyone who has truly repented. God in His divine goodness has

forgiven him all the sins he has ever committed; He will not remember them
anymore.

Jer.
31:34

But original sin remains with man; he
will not be able to get rid of it. As long as
he is in the flesh he will have to struggle
with it. God will protect him in this
sturggle if he has a horror of sin and hates
his own flesh. Never will a man who truly
fears God willfully and knowingly agree to
commit sin. He knows that he would anger
and betray his Lord. Such a man "rejects
the deeds that men hide for shame"; he
does not give in to temptation or pursue
sinful thoughts. He fears God and is
master over his own mind. We are called
not to sin but to resist sin, to repent of the
cunning of the flesh, and "to take every
thought captive to obey Christ."

2 Cor.
4:2 (NEB)

2 Cor.
10:5

We need to discern clearly that a God-
fearing man is not a sinner as long as he
does not give in to sin in his heart and does
not yield his members as instruments of
wickedness. Sin may stir powerfully in his
flesh, but he fears God and strangles his
own impulses; through the power of the

Rom.
6:13

Spirit he overcomes temptation. When that happens, sin must simply give way. The Spirit puts the works of the flesh to death so that sin cannot raise its head anymore but must come to an end with its evils works.

Indeed, they say, we are by nature children of wrath from our birth; what would happen to a child if original sin were not taken from him through baptism? Not so, we reply. Original sin is not taken from man until the grave. But we would all remain under God's wrath, had God not remembered His mercy and sent us His promised Messiah, Jesus Christ, who turned back God's anger and won His grace for us who believe in Him. This same Jesus also justifies the little children; He says they are not gulity until they start to sin. The Lord points His disciples to the little children and says, "Truly, I say to you, unless you turn and become like children, you will never enter the kingdom of heaven." "For to such belongs the kingdom of heaven."

Why then does the Lord allow it that

Eph. 2:3

Ps. 98:3

Matt. 18:3

Matt. 19:14

His faithful ones, even after the grace of forgiveness, remain so weak that they are exposed to all kinds of temptation? He does it lest they take His grace and assurance of salvation to themselves and become proud and arrogant, lest they think nothing is wrong with them and feel safe. He lets them feel their own unworthiness so that they remain humble, not becoming self-confident and relying on their own goodness, but trusting alone in Him who raises the dead. God gives His children ample cause for praying to Him from the bottom of their hearts. The weakness of the faithful thus gives cause to praise God. It makes them draw all the closer to God, and should they fall seven times in one day, they will not despair but will call upon the Lord.

But the godless, those who do not fear God, who are ensnared by sin, fall into it and remain in their wickedness. They sin wantonly and have no fear of God. They commit mortal sins and dreadful vices, which are judged by the Holy Spirit and cut man off from the Kingdom of God. Of these we read in Romans 1:18–32; 1 Corinthians 6:9,10; Galatians 6:7,8; Ephesians 5:3–13.

Written by me, Claus Felbinger (1560)

> For it is a shame even to speak of the things that they do in secret; but when anything is exposed by the light it becomes visible, for anything that becomes visible is light. Therefore it is said, "Awake, O sleeper, and arise from the dead, and Christ shall give you light."
>
> (Eph. 5:12–14)

Note to page 113:

At the council of Bern, 1585, the State Church declared: "'The main reason why so many God-fearing people, who sincerely seek Christ, are offended and withdraw from our church is the fact that vices such as adultery, avarice, cheating, usury, pride, profanity, and drunkenness are common among us.' The mandate charges even the clergy of the state church with such transgressions." John Horsch, *Mennonite History I, Mennonites in Europe*, 2nd ed. (Scottdale, PA: Mennonite Publishing House, 1950), p. 107.

CPSIA information can be obtained
at www.ICGtesting.com
Printed in the USA
JSRBC011019110822
29080JS00002B/2